MW00861957

BEST POETS OF 2015

VOL. 1

John T. Eber Sr.

MANAGING EDITOR

A publication of

Eber & Wein Publishing

Pennsylvania

Best Poets of 2015: Vol. 1
Copyright © 2015 by Eber & Wein Publishing as a compilation.

Library of Congress
Cataloging in Publication Data

ISBN 978-1-60880-453-5

Proudly manufactured in the United States of America by

Eber & Wein Publishing
Pennsylvania

A Note from the Editor . . .

Throughout the year I receive letters from today's poetic traditionalists who find it unfitting that we publish and recognize poems that do not rhyme; to many, rhyme is an essential component of a poem. These letters always draw a smile, as they remind me fondly of similar scoldings I would receive by my grandmother for using my debit card for online purchases, for permitting my son to watch Spongebob Squarepants rather than something more "appropriate" like Looney Tunes or Tom & Jerry, or for using the GPS on my cell phone when a map will get me anywhere I want to go. I would simply smile . . . and keep my rebuttal to myself. Where poetry is concerned, however, I must respectfully disagree with the arguments made in these endearing, handwritten notes that ever so gently admonish us for publishing poems and selecting winning poems that are written without end rhyme.

The truth is non-rhyming poetry, or *free verse*, not only *exists* but is alive and validated more today than ever. I hold no grudge, however, toward these voiced disputes. As a matter of fact, I have utmost respect for those poets who seek to uphold and respect the timeless, old-world style of poetry consisting of rhythm, rhyme, and meter; to write a poem in this form and write it well—free of forced rhyme, unsteady meter, and inconsistent line lengths—is not easy to do. I do, however, attempt to enlighten these poets by mentioning one name—Walt Whitman, the American modernist poet who fathered the free form style and brought about a revolution of sorts to 19th-century literary society and academia. His famous collection *Leaves of Grass*, which boldly deviates from standard rules of meter and rhyme and acceptable language and motifs, caused quite a controversy during its sporadic appearances and various editions in the mid to late 19th century. Today, however, this iconic collection—once scorned for its arbitrariness—is used all over the world as a teaching tool in the literary arts.

Since the time of Whitman, many have followed in his footsteps with this chosen style: Ezra Pound, Emily Dickinson, Wallace Stevens, D. H. Lawrence, T. S. Eliot, William Carlos Williams, Billy Collins, and former US Poet Laureates Robert Pinsky, Natasha Trethewey, and Juan Felipe Herrera just to name a few. Herrera was named US Poet Laureate in June 2015 and is the first Chicano to ever receive this honor. In comparing Herrera's work to Whitman's, James H. Billington, representing the Library of Congress, calls Herrera an "American original"; similarly to Whitman's *Leaves of Grass*, Herrera's poems "engage in a serious sense of play—in language and in image—that I feel gives them enduring power . . . I see how they champion voices, traditions and histories, as well as a cultural perspective, which is a vital part of our larger American identity."

The underscoring of the American identity in their works can only be carried out through free verse. Linear freedom of the free form style is what inspires the poetic voice to speak freely and encourages unrestrained thought. For both Whitman and Herrera, their lyrics are "freeing"—freeing of attitude, beliefs, emotions, opinions, observations, and judgements. To have all of these notions confined to a set rhythm and line length would not only produce a poem that is completely ineffective but wholly untrue. The meaning would be buried in syllables and feet, with the poem's overall purpose still begging to be released from within the poet's soul. In 1855, Whitman simply took the American credence of freedom and ran with it. Today, poets like Herrera not only carry on the American tradition of free verse style but have taken it to new, successful levels, proving further that poetic artistry can be just as pleasing to the mind as it once was to the ears and eyes.

At the very least, I hope I have persuaded many of you, formalists or not, to get to know the work of these prolific authors and become further acquainted with this contemporary, non-confining style of writing. Perhaps attempting this style will even encourage you to broaden your repertoire of themes. Don't be afraid to push yourself in surprising new directions!

Rachel Mueck
Executive Editor

Positive Truth

You can be positive
    And still tell the truth,
No matter if you're aged
    Or still in your youth.
We all can be grateful
    For so many things
No matter what
    Sorrows life brings.
In many ways we are blessed,
    But we don't have to lie.
There are times when
    We all have to cry.
Being positive is
    The best way you can be
By knowing
    "The truth will set you free."

Carol Kaufman
Portland, OR

I John 4: 12–16

Everyday we're asked to sign our
Name to I John 4: 12–16.
To make it our daily routine
Every flower is a soul blossoming,
In nature.
A bird does not sing because, it has
An answer.
It sings because it has a song.
That keeps faith sweet and strong.
The butterfly counts not months,
And has time enough,
Through these times just look, for
The sunshine
It lifts upon wings, of joy beyond
Comfort, hopes and dreams always there.
Know with our Savior at our side,
We can have a happier day.
Hold onto His hand, let Him lead
The way.
Gifts from the creator's hand
We thank and praise Him, for
Everything so grand...
For His love has made it so.

Connie R. Holt
Waynesboro, TN

I'll Love You Always

I loved you yesterday, I love you today,
I'll love you always.
You were my high school sweetheart,
My husband and my best friend.
After you had to leave us, I dreamed
We were walking hand-in-hand in a
Beautiful land, some day we will,
I'll live with my memories until then.

Bonnie Watson Jolly
Cedartown, GA

This poem was written in memory of my husband, Richard Allen Jolly. He was killed on January 27, 2015. A big truck ran a stop sign and killed him instantly. He was sixty-seven. He was also my world. We went together four years (since we were sixteen years old). We were married forty-six years. I miss and love him very much. I really dreamed, after he died, that we were walking hand-in-hand in another land. I believe that was God's way of telling me we will some day.

Happiness

What is happiness… is it having someone
who cares about you?

Is it having someone for you to love
and cherish for a lifetime?

What about someone you can stay up all
night talking with?

How about playing with family and friends?

Happiness can be many things, but most
of all… happiness shows the real you.

Kayla P. Bass
Hayfork, CA

*This poem was inspired by the love of my life, friends, as well as family. I
want to take this time to thank all of the people who support me and who
push me to do what I love. Thank you and I love you all.*

One-Sided Love

You're so good for me.
Sweetheart I'm happy just to be
Anyplace on earth with you by my side.
Heaven's what you'd be
If you just tell me you love me.
Say you need me as much as I need you.
Here I go again.
It looks as if I just can't win.
I think I'll build a fence around my heart.
I know you're not to blame
Because you just don't feel the same.
You can't help it if I fell in love with you.
One-sided love is hard for me to handle.
You never tell me that you love me too.
If you can't feel the same,
Darling, I know you're not to blame.
I can't help it if I'm so in love with you.
Here I go again.

Lawanda Gray
Pineville, LA

In a Dugout

Flames are flickering in a small stove,
Drops of resin on billets—like tears.
A harmonium sings of you low
In a dugout midst the war's fears.

On sub-Moscow snowbound fields
In the whisper of shrubs you appear.
I wish you hear my song, that reveals
How sorrow dwells in me here.

You are now so awfully far,
All the snows are between us, perhaps.
To reach you—is for me very hard,
To reach death—one needs only four steps.

Sing, harmonium, to spite the storm,
Call for happiness lacking in life.
In the chilly dugout I'm warm
Thanks to my inextinguishable love.

Emil Brainin
Pelham, AL

The Fifth Freedom

America the beautiful, America the free
USA the land of hope and opportunity
America the powerful, America the brave
The stars and stripes forever, long may Old Glory wave
These are words we hear each day and grow to understand
They're taught in every home and school all across the land
America the bountiful, enough for you and me
America the wonderful, from sea to shining sea
We learn of all our blessings that are with us every day
We're free to speak and eat and sleep and free to write and pray
Though sometimes taken for granted, they are so very dear
Freedom of speech and religion, freedom from want and fear
But there is one other freedom to be added to the four
As important and as valuable and maybe even more
Yet this freedom is the only one that some people do not use
The right to vote and to elect, the freedom we have to choose
It was written in our Constitution, three centuries ago
By the men who forged our country, by the men who made it grow
That we shall choose our leaders, they will not come by selection
They'll be for the people, by the people, chosen by election
And each and every citizen, no matter poor or rich
Can step into a voting booth and cast a ballot which
Puts in their hand the power and the might to take a stand
To choose the laws and leaders of this great and wondrous land
So to get your share of America, stand up! Reach out! Take note!
Don't miss your greatest freedom, don't miss your chance to vote

Donald Robert Stoltz
Philadelphia, PA

*Dr. Don Stoltz practiced family medicine in Philadelphia, PA, for thirty-five years. During this time he wrote twenty-one books ranging from illustrated children's books on medical subjects to a teenage novel, about a summer camp in the Catskill Mountains, to a three-volume set of books—*Normal Rockwell and the Saturday Evening Post. *He also wrote a play titled* The Waiting Room. *His book,* Classroom Times—Charactoons and Rhymes, *was chosen as the best children's book at the World Book Awards in 2012. His most recent book is* The Bubble Flight to Israel. *His biggest admirers are his seven grandchildren.*

Cabanas Tropicais

The land has been smiled upon by God
with flowing waterfalls and greenery.
The sun shines brightly and the water sparkles
like fine diamonds as it falls freely.
Cascading down the hill rushing to reach its home,
landing to awaiting creeks and rivers to forever roam
he stands at the water's edge with open arms
to reveal his secret paradise.
Welcoming everyone to taste the sweetness of it all
and willing to sacrifice.
The secret he has kept to now share
with all who seek adventure and true peace.
His smiling face and hair with hints of silver
will be waiting to hand over his showpiece.
Cabanas Tropicais is a must experience,
leaving all your cares and worries behind.
A whole new world awaits your presence
to create, relax or unwind.
On the possibilities when letting go and being renewed,
finding your child-like innocence.
To once again embrace life with passion
and fill your heart with love in abundance.
Now that's the way to spend a while in time.
Soaking up sun and healing
on God's playground is so divine.

Yolanda Orozco Mendez
Houston, TX

Yolanda Orozco Mendez's poetry has been published in several books. Poetry was her niche in "Boundaries of Romance" and it will play a big part in her upcoming book, Spiritual Portal, *due out by end of year. Poetry is a way of expressing her deep heartfelt feelings, left opened for readers to come away with a different meaning. This poem was written for a friend whose passion is his tropical oasis, an oasis he is building for the unique traveler, the traveler that desires the unordinary in traveling. The hidden gem is located in Macae, Brazil.*

Reaching Out

Reaching out in kindness, patience, love.
Reaching out in peace, but most of all
in respect.
Reaching out with an open hand, can fill
a treasure chest of many beautiful gifts.
Reaching out giving thanks to all people
who serve you, change one, and brings
a smile to that person, no matter
what walk of life they come from.
Reaching out to young and old alike shows
that you have respect for those who serve you.
Reaching out is not always easy, but with a
kind word, can change one's outlook.
Reaching out in respect, and kindness, with
a peaceful thought, could open many
doors and change the world.
Reaching out with respect can fill one's
treasure chest with many beautiful gifts
along the way of one's life.
Reaching out with respect, shows how one
cares for one another.
Reaching out is a true gift.

Carol A. Miller
Washingtonville, NY

Visiting Grandma and Doc

Fun summer evening,
As my brother Jim and I,
Down in Lewistown,
Visit Grandma and Doc,
And lounge in den at table,
Next to antique desk—cacti, house plants,
As we share stories about our family,
Their adventures in England, Ireland, Germany,
As we admire their lovely China Closets,
And they show us their rocks, coins, and stamps,
—Basement, attic collections,
While we enjoy "Lost in Space,"
Share peach pie, orange tea,
Fragrant breeze drifts through windows,
And makes wind chimes sing.

William D. Irwin
Princeton, IL

My brother, Jim, and I thank our dear Aunt Betty for helping us, motivating us and inspiring us, all of our lives (from little kids to adulthood), to make something good, positive and constructive with our lives and to be the best people we can be—being dedicated, vital and contributing members in our communities and society—as we share, with God's love and grace, our gifts, talents and aptitudes with our families, friends and everyone.

The Farmer's Wife

She grew up on a farm, where she learned to do chores.
She learned how to feed chickens, milk cows, and ride the horse.
The farm had a creek where she spent many hours.
She climbed the banks and picked berries and flowers.

Her grade school days were spent in a parochial school,
Where she studied hard and learned the Golden Rule.
She went to high school in the city, which was eight miles away.
She learned math, English, science and home ec every day.

After one year in college she made the choice to quit school.
She had a ring on her finger from a guy who was "cool."
So on the fifth day of August in 1951 at the church
She married the guy of her dreams, and he would always come first!

He was a farmer, and was looking for a farm on which to live,
The farm they found had a house, several barns and a grain bin.
They planted a garden that first summer and every year since then.
Within six years the farmer's wife had four children to tend.
The children all went to grade school and high school in the country
And attended Sunday school at church and 4-H meetings in
the county.

We won't forget the chickens, which had to be watered and fed.
The eggs needed to be gathered and the broilers had to be tended.
Or the cows that had to be fed and needed milking, morning
and night.
And the pigs that needed feeding and you hoped they wouldn't bite.

The farmer planted soybeans, corn and alfalfa hay.
The farmer and his wife worked hard every single day.
She cooked the meals, cleaned the house and sewed the clothes.
She taught her children how to practice all they know.

Carylyn E. Runge
Columbus, NE

*I am a farmer's wife and I grew up on a farm. I wrote this poem from my
lifetime experiences.*

Just a Kiss

My intentions
The romantic way
First your eyes
Tip of your nose
Your cheeks
Finally your lips
—For sure—
A kiss has a message
Of its own—when
Applied by the lips
Of your loved one
—So true—
The kiss of a woman
Can do wonders for
A man's moment to remember
—Honestly—
I love the way you
Kissed me the first time
I love the way you kiss
Me now
—Now I ask—
How many times have
We satisfied our
"imperfection"
With just a kiss

Robert I. Garcia
King City, CA

Footprints on My Heart

You have left your footprints
through many years
filled with happiness and laughter
and sadness and tears.

I held you close
when you were little boys
as I dried your tears
and shared in your joys.

I kissed your boo boos
and made them okay
as I watched you grow
day by day.

I watched over each
as the years went by.
I have many memories
that money can't buy.

Now you can see
from the very start
how you left your footprints
on my heart.

Mary Alice Seiter
Lexington, MI

Hollow...

Empty vessel
Void of life
A shell of her
Former self
Loveless and scared
Hopeless lonely no
Way out
Screaming in a
Crowded room but
No one hears silence
Deafening maddening
The aching pain
Searing piercing
Her soul endless
Torture
Dark confining
Closing in helpless
Drowning can't
Breath suffocating
The rose withers
On her stem an
Falls away crushed
Defeated gone

Rose Scott
Rochester, NY

I'm proud to be included in this compilation. My poetry means everything to me, and I hope it's enjoyed by others for some time to come. I've been writing now for a few years. I'm forty-five years old and looking forward to advancing my career as an author of my own book some day. As I perfect my craft, I get a better understanding of my gift and the world around me. It's my responsibility to be true to myself at all times as an artist.

Heartbeats

Father can you hear my heart
    beat—beating in my chest?
It's weary and it's burdened;
    my Lord, it needs to rest.
It aches to be inspired,
    set on fire once again;
To love and feel and act with zeal,
    and follow you as I intend.
I want my passion to be real,
    an intentional life restart.
My chest is thump-thumping;
    Father, can you hear my heart?

Josey Waggoner
Shoals, IN

Things Spring Brings

Sunny spring's welcome warmth is here
    after a winter cold, icy and drear.
Now soothing breeze and gentle rain.
    Hooray! It's green-up time again!
Singing birds and blooming flowers,
    I could sit, listen, watch for hours.
But I must do French calisthenics, alas,
    called "mow de lawn, coup de grass."

Philip N. Martin
Tulsa, OK

My Faith

When the storms of life
Bring trouble and strife,
Strong winds cause my frail ship to heave;
Then waves of doubt,
Cause my soul to cry out —
"Dear Lord, please help me believe!"

Then the face of my Savior I see,
And He whispers, "I am with thee.
Be it ever so dark,
Believe in your heart,
And you'll walk on the water with me!"

Betty Paschall Grantham
Grantham, NC

My husband, Jerry, and I, with our German shepherd dog, Jag, live on a beautiful horse farm that has been in Jerry's family for over two hundred years. We have been married fifty-four years, have three adult children, twelve grandchildren, and two great-grandchildren. They are scattered over the US, with one in Australia. My faith in Jesus Christ as my Lord and Savior has brought me through major heart problems and four different types of cancer (three of them in the last seven years) along with the assorted surgeries and treatments for them. He is the inspiration for this poem.

We Remember

You still make us laugh today
Though it's been over six years since you went away
We remember and talk about things in the past
In our minds those memories will always last
The memories are all good, but I still feel blue
I have the memories, I don't have you

We remember all your sayings you told us
And still crack up because they are so hilarious
Sometimes just a word or phrase or song playing
Reminds us of another humorous saying
The memories are all good it's true
I just wish I still had you

Chester Williams
Jewett City, CT

The Travelin' Man

He packs his bags for the trip ahead
Another hotel another bed
In this bed he sleeps alone
Knowing that this is far from home
He thinks of the woman that waits
About taking her on fishing dates
Finally sleep sweeps him away
Letting his body rest for the coming work day
Another job another problem
He works all day just to solve them
The day is long and the day is tough
He knows that he is looking rough
Wanting to hear her voice
Home is where he'd be if it was his choice
Stepping in the shower the water washes away the grime
Wanting to come home for some quality time
He is ready for his traveling days to end
For he wants to be with her and watch her hair blow in the wind
Truck window down on the back road
Spending time with her in cruise mode

Courtney Swanner
Newton, KS

What If...

What if kindness to others was statutory
and goodwill, benevolence were primary?
Words of hate and revenge become extinct
replaced with compassion more distinct.

What if laws were made with a purpose
that benefits mankind and not foreclose
the rights and privileges that is fair to all?
Statutes favoring special interests appall.

What if lobbyists were unable to court congress?
Perhaps citizens would experience more success
from legislation more favorable to the public.
Good laws happen when men do not politick.

What if those in power forgo self–interest,
Give others a chance to feather their nest?
Cronyism and special interests are not fair.
The poor want a chance for their fair share.

What if international wars were not permitted
and now obligatory negotiations were exacted?
How many lives and damages would be spared
to improve humanity and the planet instead?

Gordon Bangert
Vail, AZ

My poem was written not to criticize but to inspire a more friendly relationship with our fellow humans. At eighty-five years young, I have seen much technological progress. It seems relationships need to catch up.

Why Do They Call It Commencement?

Let's not accept that she cried at the end of fifth grade
Let's deny that her friends are only temporary
Let's keep the truth of her intelligence in the shade
Let's say life's still young and growing up isn't scary

Let's fool her into thinking that the movies are real
Let's distract her when she notices the dog's aging
Let's keep her innocent with a well-constructed spiel
Let's tighten the bars of ignorance that she's caged in

Let's pretend it's still August; come September she'll grow
Let's imagine it's still July; come August she'll leave
Let's continue to tell ourselves that she doesn't know
That we are her and she is me, and I am eighteen

Let's deny that it's spring and that I'm going away
Let's not accept that today's the day I graduate

Kasey Kirchner
Middlebury, IN

Angel by My Side

At the beginning of every day,
Thoughts gather to guide my way.
I feel a sense my angel is close by,
Giving a heads-up on whatever I try.
A beautiful cardinal in my backyard tree,
Chirping messages my angel sends to me.
A fascinating cloud formation up above,
Giving an overwhelming feeling of love.
A tingling sense that something is wrong,
Sending me a warning until danger is gone.
If sadness should bring darkness my way,
My angel surrounds me with hugs that day.
I'm so blessed my angel is forever near,
Whether my day brings a smile or even a tear!

Kathy O'Connor
Mahopac, NY

Loyalty Returned

Overworked and underpaid
They really think we are their maid
We are on call both night and day
To fill their needs in every way
To keep alert for every sound
Treat us with such jubilation
When we return from our own obligations
They really couldn't live on their own
So appreciate when attention is shown
Pay us back in many ways
Play upon our heartstrings every day
These canine friends so very loyal
So we really don't mind all the toil

Elizabeth Thompson
Blandburg, PA

I've owned so many different dogs — or you might say they owned me. Some come from the shelter. One dog was upstairs. I was working downstairs. She barked with no letup. I came up to see why. I checked to make sure the door was locked. The lock was loose — came out of the door. I was so thankful for her. The lock was repaired. In the morning, I found a skeleton key on the patio below.

Glory!

Out of the ashes of defeat
Came glory! Glory!
Out of the fire and smoke
Came a glorious story!

What was meant to harm,
Brought suffering and pain.
What was heralded victory,
Brought to us great gain!

For even now the cross stands
Witness to the glory—
Even now a witness shines,
Oh, witness the cross of glory!

Darlene Stewart
Independence, MO

Even though 9/11 was fourteen years ago, today, remember, there is witness of God's mercy in the 9/11 museum: a cross of two steel beams that came out of the fire and ashes. It is a witness to our foundation in this United States of America—the cross which stands forever witness to this nation's existence—to glorify the Son of God in glory, Jesus Christ.

Come See Me Again

Forgive me if I forget your name,
Today's date, events of the past.
Your presence is welcome just the same.
Oh God, help this memory last!

Come see me again!

I live here now. I'm often so lonely.
It's not my home. Where is my home?
All day they lock the doors to outside.
Do they think they feel I may roam?

Come see me again!

No one has come for a very long time.
A robin sits at my window singing.
I wish he'd stay! No, he flew away,
Happy and free in his winging.

Come see me again!

Evelyn Shriner
Lawton, OK

Dancing with Daddy

As a silly daughter,
I have a funny father.
I wiped my hands on his pants,
And he taught me how to dance.

He held my hands,
And we danced to different bands.
But before the music came to a halt,
We would always get in a waltz.

I stood on his feet,
For his eyes I could not quite meet.
With grace and patience,
We would always dance.

As I grow older,
I can now hold his shoulder.
Together, swinging and shaking,
Look at the memories we're making!

Hand in hand, we will always dance.

Tayler K. Ekness
Post Falls, ID

Gone

It's hard to fathom
   so much fervor
   and passion
      leaving no further trace
      across your memory:
absorbed like a
discarded rock
     when it sinks in silence
     through pond water —
       nothing left but
       ripples dying in
       concentric circles,
   until the surface
   has no record
      of its passing....

Judy-Suzanne Sadler
Cortez, CO

A Warm Refuge

I was lost and you found me.
Yesterday I was so hungry!
Today you feed me, and give me water.
I was hit, kicked and abused;
you took me under your care
and loved me.
Bow-wow! All kinds of dogs, cats,
and other animals are here too.
Now this is life so good!

You give me medicine when I'm sick,
you walk me for exercise,
and I have a warm bed at night.
You are all so nice here;
someday you shall find me a home.
Until then, thank you for the shelter,
the food, and your warm love.
I will always remember you
for the kindness at the shelter
along with so many others
staying here in peace. Woof!

Dedicated to Hazleton, PA, animal shelter
And shelters across our USA.

Andrew Batcho
McAdoo, PA

Crossing Over

Crossing over is expectant
At the end of each one's life
There is a peace that comes
You're ready for the flight

To loved ones of great sums
What a joy to see them there
Years without them fade
They circle everywhere

All the pain and heartaches
Left behind in a dying world
Replaced with the Word
We're there for Jesus' sake

Everyday is a little closer
To the crossing over there
My steps are getting lighter
My hopes are even brighter
I will meet Him in the air

Sally B. Ray
Palestine, TX

A Soldier's Prayer

Dear Mom,
I wish that I could be
With you on Christmas
This is a dream I share
With a million other guys
From here and everywhere
I wish the world was free
All our cares were few
As things are the way they are
Don't be sad and blue
Christmas and always
My thoughts are all with you
When you open up your gifts
On Christmas morning
Mine will be under the tree
The only thing I couldn't wrap up
Was all my love for thee
Now I hear the bugle blowing
The lights are going down low
I'll sign off with love and kisses
A merry Christmas
From your son

Joe

Catherine Marin
Bayside, NY

Bear-A-Dise

We are a country crew
Wanting visits from people — but only a few
We enjoy nature surrounding our home
Enjoy being quiet and all alone
No radios with singers rapping
Only woodpeckers doing their tapping
Setting on the deck watching a bear
Easily eating, not giving a care
There are bears inside and out
We love bears, there is no doubt
Their coat of fur ripples as they walk
They are so quiet they can even stalk
Roaming the woods looking for food to eat
When they come upon our corn — oh what a treat
They enjoy the sunflower seeds we put in our feeders
Scattered all around, couldn't they be a little neater
They make sure their little ones eat their fill
Then up they go and over the hill
Down to the stream where the water runs cool
They play around like swimming in a pool
Finding a moss covered spot
Under the trees where it isn't too hot
They all lay down together for a brief little nap
As ferns bow over their heads like tiny fuzzy caps
Our home feels so much like paradise
We decided to name it our — Bear-a-dise

Barbara Wert
Dushore, PA

I just started writing poetry about four years ago. I am a senior and recently discovered how exciting it is to write down my thoughts. I live in the country where I am surrounded by God's beautiful nature that inspires me. My father was in World War II and also wrote poetry. He would send poems home to his wife and his mother. I now dedicate this poem to my father. He was a wonderful son, husband, and father who we dearly miss. By the way, his nickname was Bear.

Looking at Ezra

Baby o' baby
What do you see —

What do you see
When you're looking at me?

What are those secrets,
Hidden deep in your eyes?
They seem so familiar
From way down, inside…

If you could just talk,
Would you tell it to me?
Or just keep me guessing
At what it might be…

But soon all your secrets,
Will fly on their way,
As you learn how to speak,
Taking secrets away…

Della Nass
Delray Beach, FL

This poem was written as I was feeding two-month-old Ezra, my great-grandson and the namesake of my late husband. He was looking straight into my eyes, as though he knew "something." The poem, "Looking At Ezra," just poured out of me and onto paper.

Alone in the Night

I know no thirst, behind this peace of mind
No familiar faces, behind this peace of mind
Abandoned trust, behind this peace of mind
Broken, death will come someday
Ill-exposed by all the lies told
Words of informality ill-imagined delusions
There must be a better place in this world
To heal the pain I now feel inside
A place where solitude solicits my tears
Solicits my fears of being touched
Not by thoughts, I felt I loved once inside
Deeply hidden rage holds a place dear to my heart
I've been raped alone in the night
My innocence exercises,
The pain, the fears, the tears I share
Holds a dangerous place inside ready to explode
I know no thirst, behind this peace of mind
No familiar faces, behind this peace of mind
Abandoned trust, behind this peace of mind
Broken, death will come someday
Hit by the bearer of my roots
No way
It came unexpected, an intrusion
I never wanted to hide
I never invited you to walk on the idea
I wanted you to have me
No not this, not like this
The memory of your breath
The heat from inside
Scatter thoughts of dead faces
Moldering imprints in my mind...

Angela Khristin Brown
Las Vegas, NV

*Sometimes the hardest thing about love is that true love can be lost forever,
and when the memories return your life will never be the same, and your
emotions from the past hold no reservation. Sometimes love is reality you need
to transform, grow and change.*

Depression

Depression is like a black hole, so hard to get through
No matter how hard you try, you still don't know what you
 should do.
You go through life doing your best for your family and friends.
Always being kind hearted and having a helping hand to lend.
You do the very best you can in every single way
But for some reason you're always the one who has to pay.
No matter how much you try you always feel as if you failed.
All it takes is something small like getting a terrifying letter in
 the mail.
Or losing the most important person in your life at the time.
The most scariest things happen at a drop of a dime
You cry where no one can see your tears.
You try so hard to hide all of your fears.
Depression keeps sucking you deep within.
You want to be the way you were in which you began.
Worrying about what's going to happen to you.
Trying to push through it, is all you can do.
It's so hard to climb that mountain to reach the top.
But breathing in that accomplishment, maybe the bad will
 finally stop.

Jessica Lynn Knight
Clinton, SC

Second Love

First love's exciting
Everything is new
You are in heaven
There's only you two

Together you know
Life will not end
When all of a sudden
You've lost your best friend

Now you're alone
What will you do?
Now there is one
Where there used to be two

God has a plan
Meant only for you
If given the chance
You'll find someone new

One day you will find
God gave you a friend
God has helped you
Your heart to mend

You won't forget
The love of your past
But your second love
Is one that will last

Kayla Kimball
Blue Earth, MN

Up to Now

No regrets *up to now*
I've learned "the hard way" one might say
Regrets crippled me for many years
Until I found AA.

I know full well for *forty-two* years, acceptance is the key
The things that happened along the way
Have made a better me.
The lessons learned through the years
Have paved my path, to find
I'm *up to now*, with the most priceless gift
Daily peace of mind.

Wealth described by many, is different for everyone
When we close our eyes at night
Our vision sometimes changes
Life is for living, yet, it's really just a game.

Play your best, with who you are
You are your own bright *shining star*
The mirror tells us in advance
We always have another chance
Don't give up… in any way.
Make the most of each given day.

Jó Ann Boggs Cordova
Hesperia, CA

Starting over in life at any given time is difficult. My good old days started in 1932 and are still going, going, going. Lessons learned along the way have been painfully costly, from a near-fatal car accident in 1948, through marriage, children, career, separations, divorces, and deaths of loved ones, including my twelve-year-old Yorkie, "Tillie B," in 2015. Each day is a true gift. I learned this valuable lesson in 1972, finally got it in 1973. Peace of mind doesn't come easy. A day at a time, I'm up to now.

A Beautiful Spring Day

The dandelions are popping up
their yellow heads
In the green grass and clover in
the fields ahead

The colorful butterflies are everywhere
as they flutter their beautiful
wings in the air

The beautiful pink and red roses
are all budding in the spring air
They will soon be opening their
blossoms there

The birds are chirping and
singing away
on such a warm, beautiful day

The world is so colorful with
its beauty everywhere
as a cool breeze fills the air

Bobbi Jo Hager
Ozark, AL

Nurses: A Dedication

Not just one but all nurses,
To me, they are simply great,
The very finest in the slate.
With kindness, charm and grace,
To their patients, a constant delight.

Their service to others, so gladly given,
Helping the sick and lonely to live.
Never too busy to answer their call,
Whenever needed, by one and by all.

They are a gift from God, to all their patients,
Too unselfish and modest to accept praise,
Kind and gentle in all of their ways.
No matter their trials, whatever they be,
They put them aside for you and me.

When they enter Heaven's gate,
Our dear Savior will say,
"Your kindness to others was a service to me
Here is your robe of white and golden crown,
This is your home where love abounds."

Emma R. Baker
Salisbury, MD

I was a nursing assistant at our local hospital, Peninsula Regional Medical Center (PRMC), for thirty-two years. Though I was not a nurse, I always admired nurses for their dedication. Now that I am eighty-eight years old and have had several hospital admissions, I can say firsthand they are the best. I was born and worked at PRMC, and I have seen it grow from a small rural hospital to the major medical center that it is now.

Please Bring My Daddy Home

I miss my daddy
tucking me into bed,
and I miss his jokes and funny faces,
during the stories that he read.

He really is a good daddy
and he misses us too.
He says so in all his letters,
so I know it's true.

I know he misses my mama.
He writes, "Give her a kiss for me."
Just before he left
he put me on his knee.

He told us to say our prayers
and not to cry,
but I saw tears in his eyes
when he hugged us all good-bye.

He has a hard job to do
so please watch over him every day.
He has to help a lot of people
who live far away.

Mama says, "You've lots of daddies
to watch over all the time."
But I hope you're specifically
watching over mine.
Please bring my daddy home.

Betty Tenney
Sterling Heights, MI

I've been writing poetry since I was a child and now I'm quite old. I'm not over the hill, but I'm getting close to the top. Since I've been here through many wars, I've thought about all the children who've missed or lost their daddies. One in particular gave me the inspiration to write this poem about his feelings.

Haystack

I stood isolated, and far afield,
From other haystacks.

I was different I was told,
One said I smelled of cow manure—
Another said mold.

I was fodder rife for criticism,
A candidate for scapegoatery and bullyism.

A mix of wheat and alfalfa blowing in an evil wind,
Every fiber of my being wanting the abuse to end.

Fed up, pissed off and quite dejected,
I was a passive-aggressive pile of damp hay—
That had been rejected.

The stabs of a pitchfork never caused me pain,
But character assassination goes against my grain.

In the final analysis when push comes to shove,
Even us haystacks need a little love.

Willi Wolfschmidt
Tucson, AZ

It's Only War

Don't cry for me, it's only war,
It took the best of me, it fractured my core.

Visions stir, wherever I close my eyes,
When the night sweats come, I emit a strangled cry.

With each loud sound, I go on alert,
I'm in the war again, in my mental hole of dirt.

Don't try to save me, I'm beyond your reach,
I'm beyond all reason, my sanctuary's besieged.

The enemy's relentless, the enemy's unseen,
The enemy's advancing, so go my tortured dreams.

Jeff Culling
Hollywood, FL

Homeless Holidays

Homeless in a shelter or sleeping on the
street,
No food, no money, no shoes to wear upon
my bare feet.

Nowhere to go from the elements of
winter cold, feeling all alone,
This unknown part of society without a
country to call home.

Many have served our country
battled on the front line,
Now living on city streets begging
most of the time.

Homeless healing with honor does
anybody really care;
With God all things are possible,
each night, I'm still a soldier
at prayer.

I hear a song celebration, "I'll Be Home
for Christmas" replays over in my mind.
Dear God please help us on Earth, to help
each other through this hard difficult
time.

Homeless healing with honor how
long will it last;
A man searching without a future
never forgets his past.

John W. Johnson
West Berlin, NJ

Moon Phase Haikus

new moon —
    geese wedge honking by,
        but I can't spot it

waxing moon —
    clouds drifting
        as more stars light up

full moon —
    even through fog and tree branches,
        shines upon my window

waning moon —
    last campfire smoke
        as red embers die out

Anthony Michael Lusardi
Rockaway Borough, NJ

Leaves

Leaves are tears shed by
trees for ages past. A winter
turned cold and with the
frost the leaves are lost.
Only to well again in spring.

Virginia McCoy
Marina Del Ray, CA

No Door

sitting by the window
on a three-legged chair
looking out at you
can you see me here
I open the window
and give it a try
I call out to you
as you come by
yes, you can see me
and you hear me too
but there is no door
for you to come through

Tzippy Gurwitz
Brooklyn, NY

Yosemite Photo

Recently I wrote a book,
with a picture on the cover.
Yosemite Valley was in that photo,
with me, and my life-long lover.

We had been married twenty-five years,
and wanted to visit that sight.
That beautiful Yosemite Valley,
where we went and stayed that night.

We tried to go, when we first got married,
but got snowed in on the way.
We got stuck and towed out of the snow,
and in a motel we had to stay.

It's always been my favorite place,
with the valley tunnel view.
You see Half Dome and El Capitan,
but the weather, we hadn't a clue.

The Falls partly frozen, the snow all around,
we weren't used to that kind of weather.
But it didn't matter how cold it would get,
as long as we were together.

There's nowhere on earth that I'd rather be,
'cause I love that beautiful scene.
That's why we went back, to capture the memories,
of the view we never had seen.

Sharon E. Olmos
Huntington Beach, CA

Mother of Jesus

The moment was one of heavenly consequence. As an aura of radiant magnificence filled the air. A serene hush was mysteriously present, with volitional rapprochement dictating utilitarianism of thought.

In an emotional state of illustrious proportion, God beckoned His flock for a gathering of righteousness, as the Holy Trinity emerged through the multicolored dawn of a new day. It would forevermore establish forgiveness through humblest endearment and sublime approach.

Thy lady in reverence bowed before the consecrated cross that bore man's salvation. Her role divine, a status of exaltation. The tears that flowed from her eyes were not of self-pity, but of an unconditional love, eternally true! They streaked her cheeks, some staining a small spot of arid soil beneath her sandals. Trembling was present, as was concentration on distant plain.

Emphasizing the importance, parenthetical thought leads way to rapturous ecstasy. "To feel pain, though possess tranquility, not touch, yet be touched," was infinitely, the charismatic adornment of a mother who has mortally lost her cherished son, Jesus Christ!

Edward A. Nicholson
Locust Valley, NY

Poetry to me is something very personal. At times a transformation takes place, putting me at the scene of the subject I'm writing about. It requires me to be obligated to those who read, and hopefully they enjoy what they're reading and eventually give constructive comments. In the past, I've submitted to Eber & Wein Publishing such poems as "Baby Seal," "Old Cat's Vague Contentment," "Boxer George—The Pet Santa," and "Potter's Field Equipoise." I received encouraging acclaim. When writing "Mother of Jesus" I realized it was different than other poems, due to its profound subject matter and dedicated following who relate to it. In 1997, I sent Mother Teresa an original draft for her opinion. She responded by returning to me an honest and positive response. This I framed and cherish dearly. She passed away shortly after. I sincerely hope "Mother of Jesus" meets with the approval of those who read it, and that I did justice and captured the emotion and vox populi of those faithful and dedicated followers, the backbone of this sensitive and extremely important religious occurrence with its sanctified impact on mankind.

Childless Mom

You can read a lot of stories
About the painful days and un-glories
Of a motherless child.

Each day is filled with pain,
Uncertainty, hardship, rain
For a motherless child.

But what about the other
Who wanted to be a mother:
The childless mom.

No kindergarten pictures
No clay figurines as fixtures
For a childless mom.

No nights spent up awake
No cupcakes for her to bake
The childless mom.

She has a different story
No wretch-ing, nor a glory
She will always be
A childless mom.

Love to give
Love to live
Live to love.

Katie Rainey
Camarillo, CA

I Love You Carmelo

Carmelo, you are a sweet angel.
Your passion runs through my veins, like hot lava.
I love you sweetheart.
Your soulful eyes speak to me.
I always feel protected by you.
It's sheer paradise when I am with you.
Especially when we make love.
Mi amorie, mi amorie baby.
Oh, how I love to be in your arms.
I love your angelic face,
And your funny charismatic personality.
I love you Carmelo more than words can say.
I miss you honey, come back to me.
Amorie, Heather.

Heather Stephanie Lewis
Cockeysville, MD

Prayer

I took a walk today,
To show me the way.
How things go in my life,
Are tending to make strife.
Somehow, the direction
Lends life to the resurrection.
Although, no one cares
To show who dares,
I need to know
So my faith will grow.
Yet, in my life's map,
I'm walking in a trap.
Not knowing how to go
High road or the low
People stop and stare
I need their prayer.

Kathy R. Hughes
Sudan, TX

Our Amazing American Flag

Our faithful flag flutters freely flapping away in the
   clear blue sky
Its vibrant colors of red, white and blue swelling up tears
   in our eyes
Hand-stitched stars shining in a circle of thirteen brought
   this nation to birth
She's since grown to exhibit fifty — expanding her
   remarkable worth
Today turmoil threatens within and without, yet she
   still proudly flies
Boldly standing as a beacon of truth in a world
   somehow twisted by lies
She's often sparked the hearts of youth who soon
   choose to defend her in war
Urgently persuading all Americans — it's freedom
   we're fighting for!
Her rustling red stripes ripple on out like blood
   spilled on overseas sand
Where men in uniform strive for freedom both
   for home and foreign land
Old Glory stands for our diligent founding fathers as we
   salute these visionary patriotic souls
So keep this "one nation under God" flying high
   on those flag poles!
Also let's not forget that awful day back on that
   horrific September eleventh
But be faithful to our beloved flag till it waves us
   on to Heaven

William H. Shuttleworth
Jacksonville, FL

My own feeble words seem much too inadequate. Therefore, may these legendary utterings of statesman and orator, Patrick Henry, on March 23, 1775, serve to rekindle our own faith and patriotism once again: "It cannot be emphasized too strongly or too often that this great nation was founded not by religionists, but by Christians, not on religion, but on the gospel of Jesus Christ. We shall not fight alone. God presides over the destinies of nations. The battle is not to the strong alone... Almighty God! Give me liberty or give me death!"

July Fourth 2015

Happy birthday America!
239 years ago you were born.
Many hardships you have faced.
Many battles you have won.
Your freedom did not come easy.
Many brave souls were wounded, many died.
They all fought to keep you free;
Gladly each one served with pride.
You have been the greatest nation,
Your democracy has outlasted most.
Many times your flag was tattered and torn;
But always mended she still waves from coast to coast.
Your brave forefathers created a new nation
Where liberty and justice for all prevails.
One nation under God you must remain
Without God, America, you will fail.
America, I am proud to call you my home!
As we celebrate our freedom on this day
Let us all stand up and bless God
Then bow and pray, for God to bless the USA.

Mary Carr
Sevierville, TN

I was so inspired by an article that I read a few years ago. I began to think how blessed America has been all these years and how blessed I am to live in a free country. I pray that the younger generations will realize that freedom is never free. It has to be earned by standing up for truth and justice for all. May God bless America and may we ever keep Old Glory waving. I love God and my country.

Due Date

Bills bills bills
Oh how I wish
They all bore another's name
Instead they pile clutter
Right in front of me
All bearing my entire full name
Like a jovial circus clown
I juggle them
From one hand
To the other
If by chance
I should drop one
Why
Magically
Before me
Appears another

Milton Morrow
Milwaukee, WI

Music, Music, Music

The star of morning made a grand entry,
chasing the shadowy night away,
Leaving in the cool and breezy air,
warming up stars for morning music.
How splendid the outdoor view,
a theater in colorful life everywhere.
From tiny voices came sound of music,
in deep, mellow, and loud tones,
sounding the grandest choir,
full of harmony and rhythm,
into heaven's microphone,
enhancing all voices with wings.
Sunshine and blue skies,
turned up the volume in a bee,
buzzing its hypnotic song,
along with a cricket, both soaring
their unique rap music together.
Music, music, music everywhere,
from all voices great and small,
each singing their best,
in "voice biz" musicals,
in spring and summer, show time.

M. Margaret Hofseth
Marysville, WA

Our Lucy Rae

Ten little fingers. Ten little toes.
Oh my goodness what a cute little nose!
There's bright shining eyes of azure blue.
There's also sweet smiles expressing love too.

There's two little ears that have heard God's voice
Saying, "As for parents, we've made a very wise choice."
There's two little arms that hold us so tight,
And there's big hugs and kisses. My what a delight!

Now time has a way of passing. Just where has it gone?
She's growing up. Our hearts she has definitely won.
She's a real dear blessing. What more can we say,
Than to thank God for giving us our precious Lucy Rae.

Florence C. Tibbs
Las Vegas, NV

Dance Girl Dance

My body is my temple
The gatekeeper is my soul
Keeping destruction at bay
And sickness on hold.

Help! My gates have been breached
My doctor says, "It's cancer
And it can't be reached."

My body is my temple
I'm not done yet.
Dance I say girl
Dance the day away.

Dance and be happy
Dance and feel good
Dance on through life
The way that you should.

Dance I say girl
Dance day and night
Don't be afraid
Dancing's alright.

Dance I say girl
Don't be uptight
Dance up a storm
And fight for your life.

Rosalyn Scarborough
Columbia, MD

On a Bed of Autumn Leaves

I am holding your hand and you are mine…
For the last time here on earth, it seems…
On a bed of late autumn leaves now brown,
Fallen and spread in layers on the ground.

The bare trees are announcing the winter months,
A dreary, cold and snowy winter soon to come;
The Christmas season will be quickly upon us,
But winter… our joy of Christmas never to come.

It was in the beginning of spring, on April 18,
We joined our hands together on the altar of God,
We made a solemn promise of eternal love;
Our marriage journey began as the sun set down.

What an incredible learning experience it has been!
Peaks and valleys, gentle climbs and precipices,
Many shining moments, darkness then followed…
My unconditional love for you never ceased to be.

On our two-day mini-honeymoon this past July,
We made plans for many more brief vacations.
We enjoyed each other in a deep, profound way,
Our souls came together as we never knew they could.

Jesus is here… He takes your hand, He guides you…
In His light He takes you to the resting place,
To God's peaceful, glorious, heavenly kingdom
Where soon our souls will be joined again
Forever to be.

Silvino R. Foglia
Jupiter, FL

Another Day

Another day has come and gone
I'm sitting in my home
thinking of life's load
wondering how I made it down
the sometimes smooth and sometimes bumpy road.

I'm thinking of what is yet to be
depicting scenes
from all my dreams
the joy, the love, the laughter, the sorrows, I mean.

I think I did it mostly right.
I know I tried with all my might
to have trust, faith and hope
no matter what the scope.

Many things were good and some bad
and sometimes things were sad.
I tried to be strong and wise
and almost never gave a sigh.

The thoughts of life run deep
and now it's time to go to sleep.

Shirley Podolsky
Palm Desert, CA

I've had an interesting and wonderful life. I've traveled the world and dabbled in most of the arts. I am now eighty-nine and traveling down a different road. I'm taking care of my beloved ninety-nine-year-old husband and running a household with caregivers. Writing keeps my mind active, and I write about things from the past as well as the present and silly ditties about nothing. My writing at this juncture in the road is a great outlet for the stress in my life, and the photography I still do brings forth the beauty in the world.

Autumn Mist

In the evening
Autumn mist
Fallen leaves
Fills the street

Dragging my feet
Through the leaves
Lost as I can be
In the autumn mist

Hanging on to memories
Of what it used to be
When I had a home
To rest my aching feet

Take it to
The Lord in prayer
For those that
Trust in Him

He will lift you
From the streets
To a home
He has for you

Walking in the
Autumn mist
He will dry
Your misty eyes

Betty R. Patterson
Goshen, IN

Spring

Hello Mother Nature!
Are you awake?
Are your buds' eyes opening
to see the dawn of a new day?

Are your leaves green?
Are the birds singing
perched on your trees?
Or, are they perhaps
flirting with the wind?

Are your flowers red, yellow,
orange or blue?
Are your cherry blossoms
white or pink?
Are you being caressed
by the falling rain
blessing the land with tears of love?
Or, are you being kissed by the sun?

Mother Nature, hello!
Welcome to spring!

Marcella White
Bronx, NY

Nature's Melody

The melody from Mother Nature's symphony
flows over me like the softly fallen leaves that
encompass my footing.
Beauteous, placate and tranquil.
Breathing in the music as the sun retreats
beyond the golden horizon.
As tones of yellow, sapphire and hazy lavender
dance aloft.
While clouds meander lazily,
playing to their own performance.
I wander amongst the spicy fragrant blossoms,
I am soothed from within my soul.
Rapture and solace fill my consciousness.
Sitting at the end of the dock,
skimming the water with my toes.
I watch as the cattails sway to and fro,
as to keep time with every note.
As the sun descends past the cottonwoods,
a mockingbird imitates in a carefree manner,
damselflies sit atop the waving grasses,
as the tunefulness accompanies the
approaching end of day.

Joann C. Martinez
Concord, CA

I've Been Hurt

I've been hurt.
You've been hurt.
We both know too well
The shock, heartbreak
Of being deceived.

Only Jesus Christ
Knows and sees the tears
Heard our prayers.
Held us up
When we were too weak
And heartbroken to stand.

"Oh Jesus, Jesus, Jesus
How can this be?
How could this happen to me?
I am thine, wholly thine
And evermore shall be.
God, my God in Jesus' name
Help me, help me, help me."

I'm anchored in Christ Jesus
My only hope is he.
Bring me through this Lord God
Bless and set me free.

Glory to God he did wonderfully
He lives in me, loving
Praying for all.
Till his face I see.

Vinnie Lee Collins
Greenville, SC

Pioneer Heritage

Our ancestors settled the High Plains,
    Battled tornados, Indians, rain.

Memories of yesteryear we'll retain;
    Their devotion we won't take in vain.

A mutual alliance they counted as gain —
    Faith they never feigned.

Hard work, innovation, they didn't disdain —
    Together their dreams they attained.

Their high ideals, legacy, we maintain;
    Their enthusiasm, creativity remain.

When sunshine goes with our grain
    We'll sing a happy unbridled refrain.

Even on a desert island far from the main
    Self-revelation one may attain.

Let's lean into a loose free rein
    To overcome a wounded warrior's pain.

Then, if a miracle happens we won't complain,
    We'll simply rejoice in spring rain.

If we follow a fantastic freight train,
    Swept up in an imaginary hurricane,
    We celebrate all they obtained
    With a musical tribute, a golden chain.

Let's dine on caviar and champagne
    While dew on dainty rosebuds is lain.

Pioneers stayed in step with the main
    To the beat of a lively refrain.

Melita Warren
Hays, KS

Desire

Desire remains strong and steady like the ocean waves. Flowing through my veins with each heartbeat, warm and delicious this ritual has stood the sands of time! As the ocean holds many secrets lost among the waves, many desires flow within the waves.

Desire: a steady wave building a storm that brings waves surging so powerful, like a tidal wave, nothing could hold it back nor should it! Nature and all its glory is unleashed for the ocean has spilled over and desire set free. Waves return to their gentle flow keeping secrets with the sands of time.

Desire flows through my veins as thoughts unfold and waves come crashing in. Stronger with each heartbeat til waves flow steady and all my secrets unfold. Like the ocean warm and strong a gentle and peaceful ritual, remains!

Debra Knapp
Ocala, FL

The Bridge Is Out to Sometime

Whatever you want to do,
Can be done when you know how.
The bridge is out to sometime,
There's a solid path to now.

A thought is sent to urge you,
Toward acting on it today.
The thought is the beginning,
Now don't let it dart away.

Take your thought and go with it,
It's easier than it seems,
You put forth far more effort,
Putting off your dream of dreams.

Zero in on what you want,
It is yours, you now know how.
The bridge is out to sometime,
There's a solid path to now!

Lavaughn Ogren
Torrance, CA

Decay

Massive red brick structures disintegrating
Among the decay in the background
The passing of a unique Victorian era
Cracking white, yellow, blue paint
Chipping away consistently with age
Till only wilted remnants cling on
Dripping morning rain with overgrown grass
As the lots are vacant side by side
Where have all these giant buildings gone
Blossoms emerge from the boarded homes
The only sign that life existed before
The bricks crumble out toppling over
And voices from previous generations
Utter echoes of mourning through the rumbles

Renata Dawidowicz
Madison Heights, MI

To a Friend

A friend is one who listens
With an open mind and heart.
It's someone you will recognize
As true right from the start.

Someone you can confide in
Is a special friend indeed—
He laughs at all your jokes
And offers counsel when there's need.

A friend will not betray you,
He will guard your secrets well,
He listens with compassion
And your tears he helps dispel.

He does you many favors,
Wanting nothing in return;
A friend can hear your problems
And show genuine concern.

I'm glad to have a friend like you,
They're few and far between,
So thanks for all your help and
For just being "on the scene."

Marianne Y. Gordon
Hernando, MS

Looking Out My Window

I am looking out my window
just at the break of dawn.
I see a beautiful scenery
that God has painted alone.

I see the trees are waving.
They point up to the sky.
It looks as if they want attention
to someone passing by.

The flowers are a striking beauty.
God touched them all with care.
They are a perfect creation.
I feel God's presence here.

I see the birds are flying
up in the sky so high.
I think they are looking for a place
to build a nest and take a rest,
where the surroundings are quiet,
for the little ones must sleep at night.

I am looking out my window
thinking it won't be long
when all this beauty will be gone.
But there is another spring that follows,
and a new growth will be born.
It's a way God shows us,
There's always a new birth at dawn.

Jewel A. Durham
Littlefield, TX

I am an eighty-seven-year-old mother, grandmother, great-grandmother and soon to be great-great-grandmother. I have been blessed from everyone in the family. They are a great inspiration to me. Every morning I get up, I go to the kitchen window and see the birds and squirrels working, all the different trees waving, the beautiful flowers. So a title to a poem came to my attention, "Looking Out My Window." From this title, I wrote the poem. It's wonderful to write a poem from God's creation. All good things come from God.

God's Infinite Plan

To succeed, with His infinite planning
God rules, with loving commend
With gestures, far surpassing
All we can comprehend
And the fearless, shall be bowing
And the believers' heads, shall bend
And those, that might be doubting
Shall come to understand
That all, who are lovingly breathing
Hope, into quivering men
Shall tread, with God's all consuming
Love, on His promised land
And heaven, shall be their shelter
While on earth, we prepare, to confront
All that we shall encounter
And all, that we'll leave behind
For if heart, and soul, and conscience
Synchronize to be one, we shall find
That with this completed submission
Our existence shall grow beyond
Our feeble mortality
Into God's blessed eternity

Ute Dahmen-Burns
Kerrville, TX

Life's Pattern

There are many lovely verses
and a lot of poetic rhymes
written for some special reason or
some very special time.

But too often things that matter
often small things from the heart,
never seem to be spoken
be it time or miles apart.

So, I thought I'd change the
pattern and just say a thing or two,
about the way we treat each other
and the things we say and do.

You know it's very easy
just to smile and say, "Hello."
Just that thoughtful kind of expression
could make worries seem to go.

So let your friends and family
know "today" just how you feel,
not tomorrow or the next day
for "life's pattern" must be real!

La Rue Mumaw
Apollo, PA

Goddess of Light and Dreams

Morning glory meets sky and first light touches shadow
When one discovers a moonbeam left over from an evening dream.
Night's face then fades from view and
Becomes at one with morning dew
Where a black and white feline goddess
Divides time between the pastoral and divine.
Instead of sitting upon the pale crescent of the moon you see,
Bastet hides behind the trunk of a moss covered tree.
She searches for prey amidst enchanted moonflowers and leaves
But moves from the scene as if she has had enough it seems.
She wanders away amidst fields flooded with sunshine and peace,
Where there is no need to hunt or even look for a treat.

Gail Logan
Macon, GA

Purple Flowers

Purple flowers in the valley,
Purple hearts rest just below.
One by one we watch them bloom,
Our lady weeps where purple flowers grow.
Purple rainbow over the valley,
Protect's our lady far below.
A purple sacrifice,
Holding back the thunder.
One can't help but wonder,
How many more must grow!

Dedicated to all
The service men and women
Of the United State's armed forces.

Greg Werkmeister
Williston, ND

Convergence

Instruments and notes each with sounds of their own
Artistically combined they converge into a fabric of
Beautiful thoughts, images, and feelings of;
Happiness, sadness, love, longing, playing in the surf;
Hiking a mountain meadow, strolling in the forest;
Dancing across the ball room;
Gazing at the stars in a cobalt sky;
Watching a beautiful sunrise or sunset;

Enjoying children romping and playing;
Feeling the deep love and warmth of
Children and grandchildren snuggle in one's lap;
Realizing beautiful love has wandered into one's life;
Deep feelings of helplessness and loss as one
Experiences the death of a loved one;
The elation of experiencing the birth of a child;

Hearing and feeling the loud rumble of thunder or
Canons exploding in battle;
The calm sereness of floating on a mountain lake
Under sunny blue skies;
All this converging in one's head and heart.

Dale O. McCoy
Denver, CO

I enjoy observing and contemplating the many aspects of life, then playing with words to try and capture the essence of that which I am observing. This poem was written from the song "Convergence" on a CD The Sounds of Color *by Local Color, a Denver based instrumental group.*

The Tower of Babel

The confusion of tongues
Why did He make everyone on earth speak a single language when
He created the world?
Is the Tower of Babel to be punished, for it destroyed His gift to
mankind?
Who made Him so furious that He decided to confuse the language
of all the earth?
Was it the descendants of Noah who started to build a tower
whose top was to be in the heavens? Was it the competition
between Him and humans that turned His gifts to mankind into a
harsh punishment, which made us spend years and years of toil to
learn different languages?
What incited them to settle in Shinar and what excited their curiosity
to build a city with a tower that would reach to the heavens?
How could we go back to the first language used by Him, Adam
and Eve so that we could speak the same language again?
His fury came down, confusing "nasal stops with oral stops,"
"fricatives with glides," and "liquids with affricates." Is the Tower
of Babel to be blamed for this confusion?
No matter which we may believe in, divine or human origin of
language, could we strive to discover a way to go back to the first
language so that we could be freed from the mental gymnastics of
learning different languages?

Andrew K. Ha
Gibbstown, NJ

*This poem attempts to graft "The Tower of Babel" (Genesis 11:1–9) onto the
linguistic inquiry into the origin of language. I hope that this poem could provoke
the readers of this poem to start making scholarly investigations into the origin of
language. The debate on this issue is still unsettled and it continues. Do we believe
that "human origin is language origin?" Or do we agree that "language just
happened?" If you do not support these hypothetical theories, you may wish to take
a defiant attitude toward the existing theories of the origin of human language.*

George

George, I love you and I always will,
We are together for life,
My happiness with you,
And that is the way it will be.
I will be your love till the end of time,
No one else can take your place,
It was first romance
Five months together,
And married, happy as can be.

We met on April Fools' Day,
What a great day to meet.
It is one day to remember
And I will never forget.
Memories will last,
I will never forget the past.

Loretta Aul
Belle Vernon, PA

Forever

As today becomes tomorrow
   As the final curtain falls
Precious memories flood our bodies
   Things forgotten it recalls

That first meeting, pleasant greeting
   Angry quarrel, your first kiss
   Work and worry, hurry hurry
Things you never thought you'd miss

Clothes he wore, that silly laughter
How he combed his thinning hair
   Didn't think not for a moment
      That he would not be there

All the good times and the bad times
   Wrapped up in a mangled mess
Times you traveled, came unraveled
   How he loved you in that dress

How to carry on without him
   Can I do it you will say
Drawing strength from what and where
   Now part of me has gone away

Jo Ann Blunkall
Paonoia, CO

My Daughter Journey

March 26, 2015 was my most horrible day
when I went into my living room and saw my
daughter still sitting there
I knew something wasn't right
Because she hadn't been to bed all night

I went over to her and looked in her eyes
Her eyes weren't focused and that was a surprise
She didn't respond when I called her name
Something was wrong and that was a shame
So I called her sister she was here quick as a wink
she called the ambulance no time to think

To a prestigious hospital in Houston she went
Her sister stayed with her
The ER doctors, nurses and staff took care of my daughter as if
they were heaven-sent
We were told my daughter did not have a heart attack or a stroke
However she was seriously ill and that is no joke

A new medicine the doctors found
To which with good results my daughter did respond
My daughter was discharged from the hospital April 16, 2015
that pleased her family
She is still under the doctor's care and they are happy
However she is regaining her health but it's a slow recovery

Burnardine Flanagan
Houston, TX

I Am Wild

Breathe fire
Stardust crusts
My rolling eye

Shake the dirt
From my fur
Carrion in my teeth

My black raven feathers
Rain upon the earth
Beneath me

I am wind
Ravenous for the flesh
Of earth and trees

My talons tear
I screech
A perpetual hunger

Carves the waves
Claw the sky
I howl —
I am wild

Lena N. Bugriyev
Roseville, CA

Jackson Ohio Apple Festivals

In the 1950s I marched in a 2nd grade parade…
A few years later, I rode the same "Mound St.
Elementary" Float! Several years' festival thrills
Was my silver necklaces; and sweetened things;
In time I rode big rides—the Tilt-a-Whirl
Was my delight; whether it was by day or
Night! But that was when I was a brave
Teenage girl! In 1966, I worked at a hot
dog booth. Then many years later I won a
stuffed buffalo! All of that was decades
Ago! Then this past September, 2014, I got
To vacation there. It's a vacation I shall
Always remember. The musical sounds
And sights of rides—plus band parades with
Miles of floats; with such rhythms of music
Notes! Also dolls I bought were special
Things I got! I rode the big Ferris Wheel
For the first time in many years! It was
Genuine like a magnificent dream—while on
Other rides some "giggled laughs and screams!"
I sang karaokes on a 2nd stage—"New York, NY"—
"Stand by Your Man," "Paper Roses," and "The Wonder of You!"
I put my heart in every song. Vacation thrills make
Me "hope" to move there somewhere to enjoy life many ways!

Frances Elaine Camp
Americus, GA

*Dad, Emory Newman, worked for Desert Farms of Cobb, GA, in the early 1960s.
I visited him six months until Mom had him return me to Ohio by August, 1962.
I lost contact with his friends and their friends—also of Turner AFB in Albany,
GA. Mom lived down the street from the September Apple Festivals. My parents
passed away in the late 1990s in different Ohio counties. If at all possible, I'd like
to hear from, or of, our 1962 friends. I'm a widow on Post Way Street. Thinking
of folks makes me want to see them again.*

Of Ships and Seas

Of ships and seas, and ceilings white,
worn, and cracked with age,
only one great hand can turn the page,
and offer true grace for the coming days,
as we wage the war in longing hearts!
For even life can seem so trite,
when sentiments do wane and ebb about,
for our seasons change so rapidly now,
the movement of the heart is so forced to run,
to catch the morsels from heaven's bounty land,
in clouds of peace and rosy art,
in gardens where we seek a start,
for colors' sake, or just to ease the stakes of risk,
from the boats sailing on, oh so fast,
floating by, aimlessly adrift,
and us, so confused in their wake...

Gregory L. Smith
Warr Acres, OK

I Am Here

Look around you, my child,
Are you looking for me?
I am here my child,
Look up in the tree.

Those leaves wave, Hello,
So you know I am here
And the birds build a home
In my branches, yet near.

Do you feel the breeze on
Your nose and your face?
That is me, my child, with
Hugs, kisses and grace.

I am here little one, on
The faces of friends, in the warm smiles of staff,
Each other, and, why, even the wagging of dogs
Fluffy tails, in the songs of the birds and in those
Big white sails.

I am here, I am near, with
forgiveness and light. I am
here, little one, in the morning
and night. I love you! You are mine! Forever!

> I am here.
> Love,
> God.

Anne M. Vannatta
Great Falls, MT

Requiem for Annie

Where did you go, dearest Annie
when you crossed life's fertile field?
Did you go around this golden pond
across the vast sea of troubled years?
You must be thrilled, dearest Annie
at last, to know your father's face
Decided your path, never looked back
you've finished running your race
No hills left to climb, dearest Annie
you've excelled life's greatest test
No tears of sorrow need you repine
God knows you've earned your rest
You're almost home, dearest Annie
you've just crossed life's great divide
A place where heavenly angels play
a wondrous place where God abides
Your sisters are here, dearest Annie
just beyond the crest of the next rise
Their radiance is like eternal sunshine
the light of love shines in their eyes
You're home, dearest Annie
you're home

Donnell Perryman
Reno, NV

Be the Change

Life goes on
Day by day.
The same schedule,
The routine continues,
A repeat of places and faces.
Why not be different
And alter the course?
Paradigm your view!
Shift your attitude!
Change yourself
To what you want to be
And open up a new world!

Joyce Bogdan
West Hartford, CT

This poem was inspired by the quote, "Be the change you want to see in the world," by Mahatma Gandhi.

Growing

All around me
It's a changing.
The color green
Is everywhere.
A flower short
And one so tall
Make life in spring
Best of all!
A grandson
Looking down on us,
As he's off to
Drive the car!
Or granddaughter
Running fast in T-ball.
A family picture
Tells it's true.
Grandson tall
As Pa Pa,
And clothes
Don't fit grandson
Like they used to!

Dorothy Justesen
Albert Lea, MN

Dearest Friend

Your name is on the touchstone
of my heart.
We are kindred spirits —
our heartstrings are tied
in an eternal linking.
Wherever we are, near or far,
when a brief thought of the other comes to mind,
we feel each other's spirit in our presence.
Before and beyond the curtains of time,
we have shared the "knowing"
of each other,
and have met in this life on Earth
to share and appreciate the greatness
of our universe,
and its mighty creator,
Jesus the Christ, our Savior and king,
Son of our heavenly Father,
our elder brother who communicates with us
by way of the Holy Spirit, our comforter,
who in turn brings to us universal knowing.
Namaste —
"I see the greatness in you,
you see the greatness in me."

Judy E. Russell
Hartford, KY

The Sea

In the midst of the sea
How magnificent it seems to be
With all its shapes and sizes.
From far and wide
In which creatures abide.
From corals to ice
To the small and to the great.
The sea in all its splendor.
How magnificent!

Dorothy Safko
Harrisburg, PA

It's God's handy work.

Plant a Seed in Your Heart

If you plant honest, you'll reap trust.
If you plant goodness, you'll reap friends.
If you plant humility, you'll reap greatness.
If you plant perseverance, you'll reap contentment.
If you plant consideration, you'll reap perspective.
If you plant hard work, you'll reap success.
If you plant a seed, you'll reap a harvest.
If you plant forgiveness, you'll reap reconciliation.
What you plant now will determine what you'll reap later.

Fred Cato Jr.
Casa Grande, AZ

Voluptuous Beauty

Having a wife can
Make your life better.
They protect you and
Share your life with you.

The righteous woman gives
A man someone to love
Giving him joy,
Comfort and companionship.

She is 39, 5-foot-7, 36-30-39
Full bodied virgin and slender with curves
With a winning smile
And a pleasing personality.

She is seasoned and wise
A woman of independent means
Kind, joyful and discerning
Beautiful with a good figure.

She has attained the measure of
The stature of the fullness of Christ
That she might be holy and blameless
Her garments are merely wheaten.

Charles Andrew Campbell
Montgomery, AL

I was born in Dallas, TX, and also lived in Montgomery, AL, and Farmer's Branch, TX. I attended several schools as my father's work took him back and forth over many decades. I was baptized for the remission of my sins in 1959 at age ten and was added to the Lord's church. I was blessed to have good parents and a mother who enjoyed doing good for her children. Life has not always been easy. I went through many trials and tribulations and made many mistakes. One of my many doctors remarked that I had a good mind and he wanted me to be able to use it. My parents returned to Montgomery in 1969 where my father retired and died. My mother died seventeen years later and my older sister in 2013. I had intended to take up writing as my career in life, and in retrospect photography and illustrating, but such was not my lot.

Awake or Sleeping

Is the sun awake, or sleeping?
Looking for a friendly smile
But the clouds just like a blanket
Keep it hidden for a while
It's Sunday morning and I'm hearing
Church bells in the distance ring
Sun's still sleeping, maybe hiding
While the children's choir sings
Must have heard the children's chorus
Come wake up, it's getting late
Push the fluffy clouds around you
From your comfy feather bed
Half awake, a ray kept piercing
Peeking with one open eye
Soon the clouds kept gently shifting
To reveal a blazing sky
With a warmth to comfort people
Dancing rays to heal the land
Meadows, flowers start a waving
Trees are busy clapping hands
All the Earth is now rejoicing
Seeds start sprouting in a row
God rules every thing's so perfect
In His love all nature grows

Caecilia DiMartino
Ocala, FL

The author, C. D. M., was born and schooled in Linz-Austria. Her father was a French Foreign Legionnaire (Charles Hainzl). After her father's death, she inherited a French villa, a house of stone and slate built in 1600, which she converted into an art gallery and school. She taught "Gift of Nature Workshops" to young and old for over twenty summers. Writing poetry is her more recent expression, because storing thousands of poems is easier than housing her paintings that have decorated her other homes and been sold all over the world. She is multilingual and has studied fine art with Claire Romano at Pratt in New York City and Normal Rockwell, among others. Her love for poetry is a gift of God, for she cannot take credit for the easy and effortless flow of His prompting. As a missionary to Europe, the author has wonderful testimonies of healing and His divine goodness and faithfulness to mankind, especially to her family. Her husband, now deceased, was a minister. They have four children and seventeen grandchildren.

Forgiveness Brings Love

As I look at you Mom in the hospital
bed, I don't see the abuse, I don't see
the bad that I had gone through
growing up that made me mad all the time.
I suffered deeply by your hands,
but now watching you in that bed
you would think that I would want you
to suffer and pay for all the hurt you caused me.
But God's grace and forgiveness helps
me face you with the love of God.
The pain is gone, it is replaced
with the rain of God's love.
So day after day I pray that you
get well, day after day I say I love you.
And show you compassion, as I wheel
you into the dining room to have your
dinner, then smile at you and tell
you that you are a winner.
The more I see you, the more my
love for you grows deeper.
I bring you gifts, you smile and
laugh and say I love you.
Now I bring you back to your room, roll down the shades,
and put you to bed, and say, Good night, I love you.

Margo Pennella
Jackson, NJ

*What inspired me to write this poem was the deep love I felt for my mom while being
with her at the hospital and in rehab. I was abused as a child growing up and never
heard the words "I love you" from Mom. So I didn't feel much love for my mom
when I was older. I did forgive my mom and learned to love her—but being with
her day after day in the hospital and rehab, there came a strong powerful love and
forgiveness towards my mom. And it grew daily. I have never felt this connection
before with her. It was a new love God put into my heart for her. Love heals all
wounds, love conquers all. Love is the greatest gift we can give one to another.*

Dreams Becoming Reality

When I see your smile, I see the sun
Why the sun you may ponder?
Since like the sun, your smile brightens my day.

When I look into your eyes, I see the stars.
You may wonder, why the stars?
Whereas like the stars, your eyes glitter with hope.

When I hear your voice, I hear the ocean.
Why do I hear the ocean you may ponder?
Considering like the ocean, your voice calms my frustrations.

When I feel your touch, I feel safe.
You may wonder, why I feel safe?
For the reason that with one touch you make all my fears dissipate.

When I am with you, my soul is incandescently elated.
I feel as if we are the only two people in this entire world;
but more importantly, I foresee all my dreams becoming reality.

Ayla Isaly
Powhatan Point, OH

Every now and then I get inspired and a poem evolves. "Dreams Becoming Reality" was inspired by the love of my life, my fiancé Gavin Cooper. He completes me and is my best friend, and on our four-year anniversary this year, October 9, 2015, we will start the rest of our lives together as Mr. and Mrs. Gavin Cooper. This poem is the first of many that a lifetime with him will inspire.

I Shine No Badges

I stand apart to serve no master,
This unmarked heathen amongst the rabble.
I work for mine and mine alone,
Without bridle, bit or collar.
This simple man, this plain brown wrapper,
An unmasked hero of the modern drama.
I wear no labels, post no bills,
My skin is bare, I shine no badges.
A web of mandates clings to some,
But not this man who leads himself.
I worship only the art of life,
And not the idols of false pretense.
Bury your symbols of sovereign regime,
They do not give me a moment's pause.
I salute no maker, curry no favor,
My slate is clean, I shine no badges.
This hurried world can pass me by.
I'll make my way in my own good time.
The dotted highways run at speed.
My patient ventures grant relief.
All the people of this worn-out world,
Carry their burdens to hearth and home.
I take no prisoners, ask no quarter,
My duty is done, I shine no badges.

George Richard Lund
Dundalk, MD

Just for Me

Oh how I miss him in the winter
but he's faithful to return each spring.
He's my little mocking bird
and he comes to dance and sing.

When I awaken each morning,
and go to run water for my tea,
I look out my window,
and he's waiting just for me.

He sings and dances his little ballet
staged atop a utility pole.
To perform just for me,
seems to be his daily goal.

He sings and he sings
and he's never off-key.
How wonderful that he comes
and performs just for me.

What? He has a feathered friend!
No! *This just can't be!*
All the time he was performing for her
and I thought it was just for me!

Rose Dyess Anderson
Ellisville, MS

I was born in Laurel, MS, on December 24, 1941, the daughter of James Lamar Dyess and Mildred Moore Dyess. I married Rushel Talmadge Anderson Jr., and am the mother of one son, Joel Alan Anderson, and the grandparent of Trevor, Jordan, Joshua and Gunter. I graduated from Ellisville High School and William Carey College. I completed graduate classes at the University of Southern Mississippi and attended the Summer Writing Institute at Alcorn University, Bill Martin Pathways to Literacy Conference, and Novel Ideas Writing Workshop at University of Mississippi. I taught for thirty-six years in Natchez-Adams Public Schools in Natchez, MS.

Can't Have It All

My best friend asked me, what do you want in a man
I gave her my requirement list, she said you'll never land
A man like that, your list is too tough
I answered her back a little bit rough
Told her I can pick and choose what I want
'Cause the need to have a man in my life I don't
He must love cats, be gentle and kind
If he isn't a model type, that I don't mind
He should like to dance, have a job, tell no lies
With hair that is dark, but he can't have brown eyes
Then wouldn't you know it a man I then met
The more that we talked the further I set
My sights on him for he had my attention
The attraction to him was too much to mention
He's attentive, notices my clothes and things
Even comments about my jewelry rings
He likes and has cats and feeds the wild deer
There's a ray of sunshine in my world when he's near
When I looked at his eyes some requirements dropped down
For they weren't green or blue, but very dark brown
The more we see each other the closer we seem to get
I'm praying that he'll fall for me, but he hasn't fallen yet
Sometimes we have to do a re-evaluation
Of the entire package that could cause elation
He says he has a girlfriend, but I'm hoping he will see
The only woman who can make his life complete is me

Jill M. Langley
Reidsville, NC

My sweet mother, who I lost on Easter Sunday, was my inspiration in all that I did. We laughed, talked and shared things that I didn't share with others. To my mother, I dedicate this poem, and to her I will remember her advice and always honor her precious memory. I love you, Mom, and miss you.

My Daddy

I know all daddies are special
Just put mine to the test
You will have to agree with me
God gave me the very best

He has patience of a saint
He was sweet, warm and kind
You could search the world over
A better man you'd never find

He loved to tell us stories
We loved to hear them too
I'll tell you this for certain
Daddies like him are too few

The love for my precious daddy
Is something you cannot measure
The thought of all my memories
Is something I'll always treasure

Violet Bennin
Shawano, WI

On Her Wedding Day

The sun, it shone bright on her wedding day
The bride and her maids dressed in leisurely way
A few glasses of wine amidst whispers and blushes
Then prepped and perfumed, to the church she soon rushes

The sun is just setting through the old stained glass
And the love in Christ's eyes seems to fall on the lass
At the flower-strewn altar stands the proud bridegroom
Friends and relatives scattered throughout the hushed room

Up the aisle come the maids, a guitar softly playing
Then enters the bride, her silk skirts gently swaying
As she glides down the aisle on her father's strong arm
She knows her beloved will shield her from harm

She feels overwhelmed by the depth of her love
As together they kneel while they're blessed from above
Then rising as one, their love sealed with a kiss
Arm and arm they depart to find their wedded bliss

Janet Sue Deckard
Texas City, TX

A Returning Servant

For the angels that walk among us,
As the doors of Heaven open,
To receive a child at life's end.
When you walk into that light,
And Jesus says, well done
Good and faithful servant,
It is then you know that all was worth it.
The pain, trials and tears,
The Lord you served was worth it all.
With his arms wide open,
And seeing his smile: you have come home.

Shirley Margaret Harding
McNeal, AZ

I dedicated this poem to Pam Sanders. We worked together for twenty-four years. We retired together. She taught for forty-seven years. A wonderful teacher, she was dedicated to her work. She also was an administrator to Double Adobe School. She is loved and missed by all of us. She went to be with the Lord May of 2015.

Monsters: Drug Addicts

Monsters hide in plain sight and snort.
They stagger around in the sunlight,
Like zombies, they're the creatures that slight.
Maybe your brother, your sister or even your mother
Are windup toys waiting until night
To give us our greatest living fright!
You hear girlfriends say to their boyfriends,
If he or she had a brain, they be certifiably insane.
And you, my dear, don't stand a chance in the heat
Of some nightmare when the loonies come calling:
Do you feel it? Love, that death inside your heart?
Do you hear it? That knocking asking to be let out?
That terrible, terrible urge to commit mayhem?
Oh, my friend! Indeed I have witnessed the strange—
And in daylight laughed—or even smiled—just child's play.
It'll always go away, when we look the other way.
Or cover our heads and stuff our ears with cotton.
You pull wings off of butterflies,
You kill ladybugs that fly into your house,
You break all the rules for gore and carnage;
You watch late night movies that scare you witless.
But everyone has a vampire hanging about,
Everyone has a zombie working late at night,
And each of us make sweet, sweet love till light
Fades, and they crawl out, till they crawl out!

Lonnie Bailey
Pineville, WV

Good Boy Rocky

My bassett hound Rocky caught a mouse,
It was hiding in the leaves beside the house.
What a mighty hunter I thought he was.
But when I looked to see what was the buzz:

I was shocked it had him jump and spring.
The silly dog was afraid of such a little thing.

He barked and howled and sang his song.
I looked around to see what was wrong.
He scratched the leaves, ran back and forth.
The way he carried on, I laughed and laughed,

Then, when I looked I saw a tiny tail in tow,
   …Just hanging out his mouth,
      …And wiggling to and fro…

Kathy A. Mathews
Claremore, OK

I grew up in Claremore, OK, the home of legendary Will Rogers. After living in Houston, TX, for twelve years, I returned to my hometown where we now reside. I began to write my poetry after retirement, as a bookkeeper at age sixty, and enjoy sharing it with my friends and family. I was glad to return to this area where so many of our school friends still live. My inspiration was the joy of living in the country and my adopted dog, Rocky, whom we cherished.

Tom

Once in a lifetime someone comes along
As soon as you meet in your heart there's a song.

Through hardships and pain he was by my side,
To comfort, support and always by me abide.

God blessed us with two children — a girl and a boy,
Now four grandchildren that bring us such joy.

I'll forever be thankful to God above,
For the life this man has given me,
And the way he has loved.

Once in a lifetime someone comes along,
And after a lifetime together — there is still a song.

Marshelle Carberry
Fresno, CA

Wonder and Delight

Fifty years of wonder and
delight.
When we first met who
would know how much
love, laughter, hope and
delight we would have.
Time has gone by so quickly,
that it seems just like yesterday
we were young and full of
wonder and delight.
With every limp and
wrinkle we still have
that wonder and delight.

Virginia L. Stefan
Charleroi, PA

Spring on Our Island

April is here and with it comes spring.
Makes me want to jump up and sing.
The snow is melting and almost no more
Now rain showers and sunshine and
Chipmunks galore.
The birds have returned so our feeders are full
Lake Michigan is waving and so beautiful.
After April comes May, it will be wonderful too.
This year, even more so, because we'll
See all of you.

Love, Grandma.

Audrey A. Beilman
Beaver Island, MI

Back on the Farm

Back on the farm
We ate dinner at noon
And supper at five o'clock
It was sometimes raccoon!

My brothers went hunting
We ate what they shot
We cooked on a woodstove
Even when weather was hot

Our toilet was an outhouse
With three holes in the seat
Took a bath in a washtub
To stay clean and neat!

Went barefoot in the summer
To save our school shoes
We ate lots of watermelon
To cure the blues

Our sweetness was honey
We had our own bees
My dad made maple syrup
From the sap from the trees

We walked two miles to school
It did us no harm
Life was pure and simple
Back on the farm!

Myrtle Batsford
Trumansburg, NY

Love Is Power

Love is the inspiring and vivacious power of life
Love has own creative power none cannot measuring it
Love able to invigorating of courage, desire and dream
Transparent love capable bringing happiness of life

Love is vivacious none cannot stop its motions
Love dwelling within love to make joyful and peaceful
Love can destroy a life and similarly can make thriving
Actives love can actualize whatever fit for the life

Love can stabilize anything by the power of love
Love has charming power life flame to make peaceful
Life always desire love — out of it none of us can active
Power of holly love easily changes obscure of life

Intentions of love life will decoration to enjoyment
Power of love able to change of fate in the earthly life
Love maintain an important rolls overall life for peace
Love — straight set all from the every corner of life

Devotion exalts love and love producing power
Basis on probity and delicacy raises power of the life
Where is love — there's the land of bliss and full of joy
Love held on power of the peace and joyful life

Love aye opens a passage for life ruin or peace
Life survive for the love and love survive by the love
Love can transform of life and nourish as one's will
Power of love can control all strife for the life

Suresh C. Halder
Hatfield, PA

True Knowledge

Knowledge, as we understand, is
learning all that's available to man.

This knowledge is confined to a three-
dimensional existence, and should be
looked upon as an analogue without
resistance.

True knowledge occurs when you enter
a depth of field beyond the third
dimension, and into a realm of
metaphysics where knowledge does
dally with comprehension.

It is a new arena that is inexplicable,
where ratiocination requires a mental
evolution for its association.

Howard H. Mackey Jr.
Edgewater, MD

Among Us

See, hear, who among us
More countless than the grasses
Or fishes in the sea
Or cattle upon the land
See, hear, what might be
More than eyes can see
Or ears can hear
Who among us knows us
What is and is not, all big and small
Should we mount like eagle's wings
And run and not grow weary
Could we search and still not know
Who it be among us, address us by name
That gives and can take away at will
We know Him as our God
As we live by faith, He is among us

Betty Shriver
Mogadore, OH

I'm no poet laureate with misspelled words and difficulty expressing my thoughts; I still love poetry. With so many good poets, I feel alone in putting to words my mind and wishes, as others have. But I'm grateful to Eber & Wein Publishing that still my poem is published.

Positive Outcome

Oh let me gently whisper into your heart
About which has set us so dearly apart!

Passion long-faded into the backdrop as a play!
Laughing in one memory, then into another betray.

My heart drifting, getting stuck hard in my throat!
Stunned silence and deep contemplation is a cloak.

Our married lifetime you demanded utter command!
Shrinking back in terror, words stung as a backhand.

Originally, I cherished you along with our vows!
I wit you snapping, loving hope from our son's brows.

I've given you my life, vigor; it's hard times I pine!
A man so fiendish, treating people so unkind.

But now is my time to regain God-given ground!
Waiting is quite frankly a deafening rip-roaring sound.

As if a servant, I dealt in strife, wasn't quite a wife!
My health waned to the point for loss in early life.

That hope to turn on an ear, you're no longer I fear!
Our adult son, you really argue as if your peer.

The attorney and laws will uphold and protect my rights!
Then I'll not be lonely at night, sleeping with lights.

With new rent-on-life, I forge forward to see,
Better chapters for both of us returning in glee!

Charlotte W. Kent
Beaverton, OR

I usually write uplifting poems for their inspiration. This poem is a tribute and understanding of why abused spouses stick out the situation in faith and in hope. Don't suffer in silence—for it is that silence which can prove detrimental. Everyone in the world should have hope, love and positive encouragement. In the case of this poem, it is saving not one, but three lives. The ending of this poem has a happy and hopeful tone—just as the situation of marriage then having a child did. Be brave and forge ahead.

Cinder Road

Early in the morning there is no rush
the dew is glistening on the raspberry bush
where radiant sun rays are shining bright
as lofty breezes take high their kite
it is the place where playful friends enjoy
romping and delighting in their summer days
this perfect love will never be rend
hopes and dreams of our future are ours always
we had our share of cinder skinned knees
skipping and prancing our lives away
fresh baked pie ice cream 'neath shady apple trees
I was so brokenhearted when we said goodbye
the Cinder Road is where you will find
whatever things are lovely and kind
the peace that passes all understandings
my dearly beloved think on those things
oh I will meet you again some day
when we will refresh and start over anew
we will forgive and forget memories of long ago
and be together again at the Cinder Road with you
come go with me to the Cinder Road
meet me there and we will dally together
frolic with me at the Cinder Road
a melody in any kind of weather
unconditionally you are part of me selfless
nothing stands in the way of our happiness

Joan Mays
West Brooklyn, IL

Thank you for the invitation to participate in poetry for 2015. Many years have passed offering interesting events that inspired writing. West Brooklyn, Illinois, became the new settlement hub of work, school and family. I encourage everyone to write about good times to help others feel better through words of comfort. Keep minds sound with Philippians 4:4–9, John 21:25 and Psalms 150:6. Other works include "Cinder Road" tales and "Rock Your Way to Heaven," a volume of songs to spur the spirit. Writing words that paint a picture and a thesaurus are tools.

Untitled

Walking the circle
I have traveled the world
I went from one port to another
I walk the circle
I return to my homeland to see my friends
When I was alone, I thought of the friends of my youth
The health I enjoyed
The nights that never ended
The surf, fun and friends
Today I am alone in a hospital bed
Thinking of my youth, my health, and the days of foolishness
Oh the circle
If I could return to my youth
Being wise knowing the word of the Lord
I may not have ended in this place
The circle
Yes, the circle took me to my homeland
The full circle my homeland

Monica Sherlock
Carpinteria, CA

I dedicate this poem to my brother, Frank, who is in an Alzheimer's ward. I'm from Fort Lauderdale, Florida. My parents are from Ireland. My mother, Kati, is from Longford, and my father, Owen, is from Monoghan. I also have a brother, Kevin, who lives in California. I'm a born-again Christian. I graduated from Santa Barbara City College. I have AA degree and a degree in multimedia. I study printmaking, bronze and wood sculpting, and creative writing. I'm a florist and a hairstylist. My poems are written to reach people to Jesus Christ.

Living in Sin

When I hear of a person living in sin, it is for sure and without
    a doubt,
That God will know and help them clean their sins out.
We were placed on earth purposely to live our Lord's way.
Certainly not for sinning and expecting to stay.
Please take our Lord to be your guide
And then you will never need to hide.

Janis B. Drinnon
Knoxville, TN

*The spiritual nature of my poems reflects my religious faith, my love of nature,
and my love for people. "Living in Sin" considers how I believe that He is a living
supreme being who loves and understands us and sees us through our most difficult
times. He Is Real, a book of my inspirational poetry and selected Bible verses, was
published at age eighty-nine by Xlibris in 2011. This new poem composed at age
ninety-two is an example of poems found in this book. Many of my poems have been
published in various anthologies and are available to read on PoetryNation.com.*

Another Poem for Steve

I'll never say, "I love you."
It isn't true.
I'll never loiter in the hall
When I hear your footsteps behind me.
I'll never feel heart lurch like a kited bird
When you cross the room.
I'll never search the crowd
For your dear face.
I'll never say, "I love you."
It isn't necessary.

Barbara Van Schermbeek
Holden, MA

Complaining

Bitterly, she complains about his complaining
Scornfully, she looks down on his grouchy moods
My patience grows thin as she criticizes him
Never aware of her own weaknesses or failings

He is frustrated about growing old and weak
He is angry about his loss of vigor
I'd love to regale her with similar woes
But God has deprived me of my complainer

Florence Pearson
New York, NY

Being Noticed

If no one were watching me live my life,
No mirror installed on the wall where I dwell,
Reflecting, responding, seeing me tell—
Then I should be pardoned for doubting my all,

Pardoned for thinking my value is nil,
For failing to honor where honor is due,
For not seeing Buddhas where Buddhas abound,
For missing the beautiful, good and the true.

We have been told that to master our fate,
We've got to incessantly search for ourselves;
Yet deep beneath everything, far underground,
There'll never be anything that can be found.

That thing that we seek is a fictional notion,
A carrot to move stubborn donkeys ahead;
But without a companion to see us in motion,
We gradually come to suspect that we're dead.

The noblest sages, exalted and wise,
Who dazzle the world with their power of light,
Require acknowledgment from other eyes,
They thrive in reflections from others' delight.

If Buddhas were Buddhas without being told,
Without someone near who has verbalized faith,
The wisdom they hold would be pallid and cold,
Dwindling down to a Cheshire-cat wraith.

Neal Donner
Los Angeles, CA

Stamp Acts

One stamp in a binder
magically came alive.

It was an Ali-Frazier
boxing commemorative stamp.

The stamp bore the word
"forever" and featured two
boxing gloves.

The stamp was very confident.
He said, "I can out lick
any stamp in this binder!"

And furthermore, "I can
stamp out any criminal
wrongdoings."

It's strange to see a stamp
eat. But this one could
gum his food.

Tom Burkacki
Hamtramck, MI

The Beggar

There was a beggar man from the Ukraine.
He played a fiddle out in the rain!
He never seems to mind the weather.
A wide smile crosses his face, his manner melts you in.
He masters this instrument with style and grace.
Destiny lays in his jar. People stop to listen, from afar.
His hair is brown and shoulder length. One can tell he is a man
of inner
strength.
Suddenly, I begin to visualize he reminds me of a familiar stranger,
one who was born in a manger.
This man appears to be at home among the poor.
He smiles as he plays this fiddle harder than before, he sits back on
a small
chair.
Perhaps I am remembering his features from an artist's conception.
Maybe I am looking into the eyes of the master of the resurrection!

Victoria A. Josephson
Melbourne, FL

Ever since I was thirteen, I enjoyed books. I have been published in Illinois, by some local newspapers, as a freelance feature writer. I love to write both children and adult stories, and especially suspense thrillers. I live in Melbourne, Florida, with my husband, Calvin, and dog, Toby. I love gatherings with my family and close friends. My love for poetry has been a growing love affair within the past ten years. I love my local scribblers writing group, where we meet and discuss local and national trends in writing. The poem "The Beggar" really did take place.

In the Moment Bereaved

Remember me in the moment bereaved
For I have lived a life-long prosperity
It was only logical
To answer the calling beyond the stars
To meet him eternally
For my time there is now

Please forgive me, dear friend
Don't shed a tear for me
In the moment of grief
For I have loved my life's worth longevity
It was only reasonable
To soar among the planets
And mingle with the solar flares
For it was time to be free

Think fondly of me
In the moment bereaved
For I have lived a life-long prosperity
It was only logical to enter
Another journey's stratosphere
And to reunite with "Scotty" and "Bones" McCoy
For they could no longer wait and linger

Chrissy Bortz
Latrobe, PA

Bonds

Bonds are formed when souls connect;
The good Lord made it so.
We meet, we laugh, we love in an instant;
Then on with life we go.
But, when I felt your heart touch mine,
I lingered on and on.
And, now the seconds have years become,
Many dusks and dawns.
I see you as my best friend,
My lover and my muse.
And, now, I bent with old age
Look back; I've paid my dues.
I ponder on life's magic;
Then with a smile and tear,
I praise my God, my Father
For giving me time here.
I thank Him for my life and love;
I thank Him for the pain,
For battles fought and wars I've lost.
But, all toward my gain.
A life lived rich and full of joy.
The hurts now count as none.
I've become that steel magnolia
I wished I would become.

B. Kay Stephens
Bessemer, AL

35 Years

You came back into my life
You had set my heart free
35 years ago
You were taken from me

I was so torn apart
Not knowing what I should do
So hurt from a broken heart
Lost and so confused

So I went to my father
This is what he did
He signed the papers for me
So I can enlist

35 years later
Here we are face to face
All the love we had lost
In two weeks, *we* had replaced

PS: My Lord, thank you for bringing
My Ginny full circle

Kenneth L. Combs
Pahrump, NV

The inspiration and words come from a love that was lost for thirty-five years, then suddenly found. The story is of my life and what made me join the Army, just to get away. The love of my life was taken away from me. We were both young and one night we got caught fooling around. I was told I will never see my Ginny again. Her parents shipped her off out of state. I went nuts. I could not stay in the town either. I had to get away. Thirty-five years later she finds me.

Poof!

People have asked me
Of my retirement:
Will I travel?
Oh yes, I tell them,
And so I have.
Each sunny day at noon
I take to my side yard
To breathe again.
I warm my body,
Listen to the birds,
Smell the flowers
And am transported through oceans
Of words
On the printed pages of books
I hold in my hands
And by the joyful songs
Of my soul.
How can I ever explain
That I have traveled so far
From the rock-hard cubicle of workaday
To that free and magical realm
I left behind years ago
In order to become
Someone I never knew?

Diane Crawford
Selden, NY

Our Tiny Little Shack

By our tiny little shack
roared a mighty river
where we'd kick back and fish for dinner.
It was rare when we got a bite
still we'd laugh and talk all night.
When daybreak came, we woke with the sun,
we worked hard all day, yet we had fun.

But, now things have changed
and there ain't no more
wakin' at dawn or fishin' at the shore.
You see, we got bored and moved to the city
it was our break in life, now ain't that a pity.
We took for granted that piece of land
that we once held in the palm of our hand.
Now it's nothing but cars that roar by our gate
and everything's split between love and hate.

Man, how I long for how it was.
Nature my neighbor and God up above.

Suzanne A. Soucy
San Jose, CA

Porcelain Dolls

Porcelain dolls all in a row
Porcelain dolls that you control
Watch them dance and hear them sing
They do what you want as you pull the strings
Porcelain dolls all dressed for show
Porcelain dolls, to you they follow
Make them break and make them heed
They won't fight 'cause they won't see
Porcelain dolls that you can use
Porcelain doll without a clue
Tell them this and tell them that
They won't chip and they won't crack
Porcelain dolls shallow and see-through
Porcelain dolls: a laugh for you
Mold 'em, shape 'em, fit 'em to a format
They think they're strong but they don't combat
Porcelain dolls not a thought in their eyes
Porcelain dolls: yes! Any other can die
Porcelain dolls 'cause they're so blind
Porcelain dolls controlling their small minds

Anastasia Luetkens
De Pere, WI

Hi, I'm Anastasia Luetkens, an aspiring author with the goal to make you think a bit more. I wrote this piece as a social commentary on how everyone does and behaves the way the media tells them to. And I know what you're thinking, why didn't I use puppets instead? Well, I used porcelain dolls for two reasons. One is that they're very pretty, and not much else. Their exterior is all they have. They're strictly artificial. And not to mention when you play with dolls you control every aspect of them, the world they live in, how they dress, what they watch, what's in, what's hot, what's not, and the dolls are perfectly okay with that.

When Innocence Flavored the Air

Childhood memories
flood my awareness,
take me to places of joy.
Times when language
was less harsh,
intent honorable,
touch gentle,
laughter often,
hurt accidental,
hugs and kisses
soothed our pain,
when innocence
flavored the air.
Initials carved in wood,
with dates, hearts,
kooky references of the times.
Snorted laughter, joyful giggles,
unbridled squeals of delight
echoed across the landscape,
coursed down the valley
as did the river at its base.
A time when future
had a naive understanding.

Ronald M. Ruble
Huron, OH

In 1946, my childhood became rural, surrounded by farming families in central Ohio, a time of being nurtured by a loving family, good friends, and happy times. We laughed, played, listened to the radio, created adventures, and worked the farm. "When Innocence Flavored the Air" is a reflection of those experiences, an awareness of how naive I was before living life altered my sense of reality. The older I become, the more I journey back to those simple days, when life seemed less harmful, dangerous, than those my grandchildren must contend with.

The Golfer

When he was twelve, with sticks
He'd hit a ball in the air —
He thought he was playing golf
Without a world of care.

A kind old doctor gave him his used clubs;
He thought he had the world in his hands.
Practicing, after getting his farm chores in Kansas done,
He'd swing and say, "I know I can!"

He was so dedicated to the game of golf
And hoped to be a "pro" some day.
Fate didn't intend that to happen
But he played all he could along the way.

He learned to "tee" off, whammy and putt
And tried his best to make "par."
His "sand shots" were good, a "birdie," he'd make
And continue to "drive" real far.

He was called into World War II.
In Normandy, he was injured three times.
Despite all of this and much more
He was highly respected as a golfer and man!

Clata Fisher
Elizabethton, TN

This poem is about my deceased husband, J. R. Fisher. He was born and raised in Kansas, then moved to Sterling, IL, where we met, married and moved to Tennessee — one and a half miles from a golf course! Later, he was called into World War II and was sent to Normandy, where his foot and leg were mutilated by the enemy. Over the years, different doctors kept telling him they would have to be removed, but with his exercising and the grace of God, they weren't. He continued playing golf — made ten hole-in-ones — and contributed much to his family and mankind.

A Beautiful Heart

A beautiful heart starts in the
gentle hands of Jesus. He shapes its
beauty with love and compassion. The
beautiful heart cries out more and
more for the touch of the master's hands.

In the master's hands, the heart
becomes a wonderful masterpiece
to work and be a servant for the
Lord God of Heaven and Earth.

Jesus uses the old holy scriptures
to be a guiding light to save the
beautiful heart, to be a sanctified light
of Christ and to receive the Holy Ghost
with power!

God called sins are the old blockage
that will kill a beautiful heart!

Maxine Harville
Bay Minette, AL

I write about things that have happened in my life. "A Beautiful Heart" was written after my heart went into A-fib. When a scan was made of my heart, the man came out of the booth with a big smile upon his face. He said, "You have a beautiful heart!" When I saw his smile, I knew the Lord had helped me, again! I like to tell about how my heart told A-fib on me, but Jesus was there to do the healing!

Exit Right

I want things neat and orderly
Like rooms and life and such.

Old Freud would say
The price I pay
For suppressed untidy thoughts.

Yet, I function better
Neatly wrapped in sweaters
Trim, tailored,
Composed and clean.

Walking amid the clutter
Of past years' struggle
Tends to lessen my present stride.

No need to tour again
Places I've been.
Adolescent adoration
Of any sensation
Promotes stagnation
And tends to hasten
A losing change to win.

The roads we take,
The roles we play,
Soon direct us more than we.
Only God need know
Or care to know
Our true authenticity.

Dianne T. Evans
Lancaster, SC

Eternal Me

Who we are is ever unique
What we are is always one
I am the eternal me
Of others there are none

The matter of life
Forever is the same
The me of who I am
Is new with every name

Our life force which is ever God
Knows best our adage true
There will never ever be
Another you

Charles O. Rand
Springerville, AZ

I am a seventy-six-year-old retired juvenile probation officer of San Francisco, CA, living in Springerville, AZ, with my wife Cristina. We have been married fifty-one years. One of our two daughters, her husband Gary and their two children live next door. I am an avocational archaeologist uncovering a prehistoric habitation site of about seventy-five rooms, with a forty-by-forty-foot prayer plaza with altar. It is open to the public for excavation, with no education or experience necessary. I hope you will join me. "Eternal Me" is everyone.

Wild

If you can't show me your love and you can't give me your
  commitment
I'll go ahead and replace your so-called pride, with pure resentment
For I don't need you, I can have any girl I choose
It's always a score for me, I can never lose
I can have anyone I want or anything I need
I don't have to hold myself back, I'll go right ahead and express my
  inner greed
For I will never have regrets on the paths that I have chosen to heed
But instead, I'll take my choice, remember it, and praise the deed
Because everything that happened was because of you and not me
For I'm glad that it's over, I finally get to be free
I can finally be my own man and not be under your control
Because you can never change me, I'll tell you right now, you'll
  never reach that goal
For when I'm not with you, I act crazy, I act wild
I won't act like an adult, I'll act like a damn child
I'll say way I please and I'll do what I want
I'll be a little pest and tease you with taunts
For I won't be all good, I'll go and be bad
I'm not the guy I said I was, I'm not the guy you once had
For no matter how many times I may sin
My cards will still play right and I will always win

Aaron Jacob Ozee
Addison, IL

Aaron Ozee is a best-selling American poet that has published nine books of poetry since 2011, writing his first collection, Celestial Inferno Poems of Another Realm, *at the age of fifteen, marking Ozee as one of the youngest authors ever to have been published in the world. To date, Ozee has made his published works available in over one hundred countries in the top three major content formats such as print books, ebooks and audio books. Visit either aaronozee.com or ozeeholdings.com for more information on Aaron Ozee and his most recent publishing and entrepreneurial ventures.*

Sparkle: The Christmas Cardinal

Christmas will be late, this year,
The word from Santa, "No holiday cheer."
His reindeer are sick, in bed with the flu.
Santa is worried and doesn't know what to do.
The elves continue to work, making the Christmas toys,
All made with love, for the good little girls and boys.
The sleigh is ready, all shiny and new,
But without the reindeer, what will we do?
When from out in the distance, from mountains so high,
Way up in a tree, almost touching the sky,
The sound of music, ringing out so clear,
From a tiny red cardinal… It's Christmas cheer!
The sound so pleasant, it makes you feel great,
Like medicine for the reindeer, it's not too late.
Her name is Sparkle, it's Santa's pet bird,
Singing the sounds of Christmas, no one has ever heard.
Can Sparkle save Christmas with her holiday cheer?
Only time will tell, as Christmas time grows near!
So Santa asks Sparkle to join him on this special night,
Keeping the reindeer happy, and Christmas magic in sight.
Singing out her songs with holiday festive joy,
Helping to save Christmas, for every girl and boy.
Perched high on the sleigh in her holiday red,
Our cardinal sings the reindeer, right out of bed.
To deliver from Santa, his gifts of peace, love and cheer,
It's Sparkle the cardinal, who saved Christmas this year!

Ed Kielkucki
Bethel, CT

Love's Fire

A raging fire starts with a spark
Like lightning from the darkened sky
One thoughtful caring word or act
Can be the spark you're looking at.

A planned event, a look, a smile
A welcome word heard for a while
A feeling that this warmth will grow
Stay here or never really know.

A heart afire and true love comes
A blessing from those distant ones
Will it now blaze forever more?
Love is a game. What is our score?

Fan that spark and make it glow
Guard that heart and watch the show
Push on so love is ever there
A fire to warm you everywhere!

Juanita Weber
Florissant, MO

What's That You Say?

What's that you say? You say there is no God?
Have you considered where we're standing now?
We stand upon the surface of a globe,
A sphere spun out into a vast abyss.
We're held down by a force called gravity,
Alone within the universe of stars.
We spin around in measured speed to give
Us night and day, while floating 'round the sun,
In season's time, we glide in mystic flight.
Located far enough that we don't burn;
Placed close enough that we don't freeze; the sun
Gives warmth and light upon the endless flow
Of life. Our world is placed within the void,
Where least amount of cosmic dust will fall,
Protecting us from tons that drift in space.
We breathe the air provided by the sea
And trees, while they absorb what we exhale.
The moon, in regulated frames of time,
Completes its cycles of infinitude,
While burning with an un-consuming fire
Of creamy light. The clouds in clusters shed
Their rain that falls upon the softly green
Hill—pastures, dells and plains, where flowers grow.
I mention just a few of His graces,
And still, I hear you say: "There is no God?"

Lynn W. Petty
Newport Beach, CA

There Is No Greater Love

A turntable bridge spanned a mighty large river.
The bridge was controlled by a constant caregiver.
The bridge was turned so ships didn't wait.
The bridge was placed so trains can pass with freight.

One evening a train came filled with women and men.
The keeper found the locks of the bridge were broken.
He must save all the people on the train.
His work must not go on in vain.

Just as the train signaled for the right of way,
The keeper heard a sound that filled him with dismay.
There in the shadows he heard his three-year-old son.
He was toddling in front of the train and couldn't run.

The keeper would hate this choice forever.
He could only make one choice, and pulled the lever.
The train's passengers continued on happily and alive,
Not knowing his son died, so they might survive.

Our God saw the world rushing to evil on sin's path.
He gave up His only Son to face Satan's wrath,
So that whoever believes in Him will not perish.
He supplies our needs, and gives us a life to cherish.

Virchel E. Wood
Redlands, CA

This poem was written from a true story. There can be no greater sorrow than to be involved in the death of your own son, yet God gave His son to die to save us. With His death, He not only saved our lives but has given us life everlasting. There can be no greater love than that given us by our heavenly Father. Yet, how often do we not accept this free gift given to us?

Dewdrops

She cried and yelled
And said, "Come quick!"
She said, "I'm really, really sick";
As she approached the hospital door,
She needed care and hugs and a lot more.

She was in excruciating pain,
But nobody believed her;
They thought it was some kind
Of game
To get a pill to relieve her.

She had been there before;
They remembered her well
How she had stood at the door
And continued to yell.

So they turned her away
On this bright sunny day,
While she cried and screamed
And tried to tell;
But nobody would listen;
So she was placed on the
Floor of a jail cell,
And dewdrops on her grave
Now glisten.

Janice R. Meyer
St. Louis, MO

I am a former English teacher and love to write. In December of 2012, I self-published a novel, A Rainbow for Ellie, *with the help of Eber & Wein Publishing. My poem is based on a true story related in* The St. Louis Post-Dispatch. *I do not recall where this happened.*

Mountain Beauty

Overlooking the beauty of a
mountain meadow lake
Fields of wildflowers spill their
fragrance with every breath you take
The beauty of the sunrise as it
lights the world below
It fills your soul with peace
as you feel its warming glow
Here the birds singing as they
greet the day
Incomparable beauty as you go
on your way
Fluffy white clouds in a clear
blue sky
Thank the Lord above for the
creation from on high

John Brannick
Colby, KS

Mama

I would brush her hair, I held
her hand, I would wet her mouth.
I would whisper in her ear, I
love you, and I would hold back my tears.
Lord, how do I deal with watching my mama
leave her earthly shell? Will I be able
to handle it or will I fail?
How do I tell her goodbye? I have to be
strong, but for how long? When can I
cry? When can I let go? Lord, I hurt so
bad, watching her slip away, wanting so
much for her to stay. I want to scream,
Mama don't leave me!
How do you say goodbye to the first person
that ever loved you? The one that carried
you for nine months, the one you are a part
of, the one you love.
You watch her breathe in and out. It is
tearing you apart. Tears burn your cheeks.
You hope when the time comes, she will go
in her sleep.
God, I feel so alone, but I know she's going home.
"I love you" were the last words I heard
her say as she drifted away.
One day I will see her again, my love,
my mama, my best friend!

Betty T. Alligood
Washington, NC

My Angel in Heaven

The smile of an angel, the heart of gold
I take after you, or so I'm told
Always willing to help anyone that comes along
I know that's right, you're my loving mom
You're in Heaven with God helping him out
I really don't know what that's all about
You gave me life to do my best
You want me strong, this is no test
When I feel low and have a frown
I think of you and turn it around
My head's held high, there is no doubt
For now I know what life's all about
You knew I could do it, now I am strong
Thank you God, I'm just like my mom

Barbara Mader
Hoxie, KS

*This poem is dedicated to my mom, my angel in Heaven. I wouldn't be
who I am today if it wasn't for her!*

MaMa

Was I a good little girl
did you remember me at all
did I laugh and smile a lot
or always seem to bawl
when I was growing up was I a tall girl for my age
did I make a small impression on you
or just race on through that stage
through those ugly teenage years
when I gave you all that
guff
did you sometimes wish I'd not been born
'cause I knew you'd had enough
when I finally moved away
did you think of me sometimes
wish that I'd come back again
'cause you see I missed you so
you were never far from mind
now you've gone this time for good
I'm an old woman now
looking back on unchangeable things
trying to sort them out somehow

Charlotte Neukam
Hanford, CA

Creativity

Creativity involves the process of having the aptitude, ability,
and capacity to use the imagination and ingenious thinking to
develop or create new, original, or unique ideas, designs, solutions,
processes, devices, or things,
and for the discovering, inventing, or contriving it brings.

Its outcomes are fresh, novel, innovative, or useful, and within a
means-ends schema, progress and change mode, it is a significant
and vital vehicle.

We tend to be the most creative by intrinsic motivation, associated
with our own interests, concerns, zeal to accept a challenge, and
sense of satisfaction.

Some people seem to be creative by extrinsic motivation,
related with external rewards, especially individuals in positions
comprising creative solutions.

Creativity is connected with divergent thinking, when faced with
a task, which generates a variety of uncommon, unusual, atypical
possibilities to unmask.

It is combined with a different organization, combination, or
unification of
cognitive elements, facilitating in the end a creative accomplishment.

Peter O. Peretti
Chicago, IL

Springtime in Heaven

I saw in my heart a picture
It was on a sad and lonely day
I was crying about my mother
Who had died and gone away.

Her body had been tired out
And worn down with age
Like flowers in the wintertime
That frosts and storms had razed.

But springtime around the corner comes
And they lift up their pretty heads
Born again with colors anew
Pinks, blues, yellows and reds.

And I saw my mother again
All fresh and young and new
Singing and happy and smiling
Like flowers with morning dew.

Mom was having springtime in Heaven
Of this I have no doubt
And then my tears were happy ones,
Thank You, Lord, I shout!

Shalom Christina Zoe
Roswell, NM

I wrote this poem as a memorial for my mother, Westa Joy Hunt (January 16, 1933 to February 7, 2015). It's only been four months since she fell asleep in Jesus. I also wrote it to give hope and encouragement to whoever reads it. Mom is not lost, she just moved to another city, and I'll see her again in the future. All people who have Jesus in their hearts have this promise from God's word. I know Mom is happy now and for that I am content. I hope you enjoyed my poem. Shalom.

My Friend

It's been a while since I saw you or spoke on the phone
with you.

I wonder how you were doing. We are both getting older and time
is slipping away.

I remember when we were young and all the crazy things we did
together.

Here I sit in church listening to your memorial service and making
sure I don't laugh out loud remembering all the things we did as
friends.

So my friend, it's been a while since I spoke to you, but in my
heart I know I will see you again. Please keep that seat next to
you open and I'll see you again, and we will laugh at all the
crazy things we did together.

Anne DeFrier
Elgin, IL

Life

One tiny handprint
One tiny footprint
A thousand memories
The dusty lane
The beaten path
Through the valley
A fragile life
Saved by "Ole Leetta"
Fears and sorrow
Brought on by war
A brother returned
Only to be lost
Daddy's darling
But Daddy went home
Beauty begets beauty
And life goes on
Two tiny handprints
Two tiny footprints

Mable Fowler
Sedalia, MO

Impatience

We push, we prod, demand to have our way;
We're sure we know the form our lives should take.
Although life's pattern changes day by day,
We're certain of the choices that we make.
We are impatient; time is speeding by.
We wish to carve our pattern into stone.
We'd see that mark remain and never die.
We want our way before our life has flown.
We have no patience for time's slow advance,
We want to have our way, and have it now!
We don't admit uncertainties of chance;
We'll make our mark upon the world somehow.
We leave behind inflexible demands,
Not carved in stone, but written in the sands.

Paul Hall
Montrose, CO

I am a traditionalist poet. I write in the rhythms and forms of the old masters. Many of my poems are sonnets. I write both Italian and Shakespearian style sonnets. This poem, "Impatience," is a Shakespearian sonnet. It is my wish that my works should be not just entertaining, but also meaningful.

Outside

Sunny days are so much fun
You can go outside and run
Run, run gals and guys
You can play and fantasize
Collect some flowers, collect some rocks
Please do not take along electronics or a clock
Run, run, run outside
Through the woods and fantasize
Keep your eyes open wide
You can play seek and hide
Hide behind a big old oak
It will serve as a secret cloak
Circle, circle 'round the tree
They will not find you, no sirree
Climb a pine tree to the top
See your world from a view that is nonstop
Miles and miles you will see
Beautiful sights that make you feel so free
Down the hill to the creek, be careful not to slide
Let Mother Nature be your guide
Go outside and have lots of fun
Be surprised how good you feel, when you are done
So, run, run, run outside

Clio H. Gerbes
Canisteo, NY

Quiet Laughter

You were a quiet person
and never said too much.
Only what you meant to
say, never in jest.
Your smile, your quiet
laughter, your eyes, always
told how you felt.
I miss your touch.
Now that you're gone, the
quietness is difficult to
bear.
Please bring back your
love, and laughter, so that
I can love again.

Jean Cast
Greenlawn, NY

Missing You

I miss you with the rising sun
    and with the fearful setting sun
I miss you during dreary days
    when consciousness of you blaze
I miss you when leaves fall
    in my solitary walks near a spacious fall
I miss you in sleepless onslaught
    when I am alone with my thought
I miss you in your distinguished days
    when in mysteries moments our souls mate
I miss you during frantic closet searches
    when I come upon your purchases

Perhaps were you be
    You are missing me?

Joseph Tuccillo
Brooklyn, NY

Rest in Peace My Love

The teardrops fall on my cheeks tonight,
As I sit by the fire and remember
The good times we shared,
And the plans we made.

You held me close and whispered words of love,
And vowed we would never part.
Tonight I sit here alone, all alone,
Remembering the love we shared.

A soldier strong and true,
Proud to serve your country,
I am proud to have known you,
Rest in peace, my love, rest in peace.

Join those that have gone before,
You will live on in the hearts
Of those that held you close,
Rest in peace, my love, rest in peace.

Linda Carmon
Cadillac, MI

Happy Birthday to You!

Children wait for each birthday—
There will be candy, presents, lots of friends!
Then they'll be teens... a driver's license on the way!
At twenty-one they will become adults—
And childhood ends.

As grown-ups we don't want to count our years...
It's better just to look much younger
And sing to others "Happy Birthday!"
Pretending that you just forgot the year
When you were born... and laugh!

But then... again a birthday means much more...
We know that God, who made the world,
Made valleys, hills and mountains of our lives,
And he alone decided ways and times for us to go
To reach the joys, the values of our earthly times.

We thank you, God, while climbing up our mountain,
Which brings us closer to the stars!
Our steps may slow, but we still climb...
No rush! Enjoy each step, each year—
The meaning of our lives!

Today we wish the joy of life to you,
While you embrace each year, each day
And climb the path, which God has chosen!
Enjoy your life! Enjoy more birthdays
And treasure each and every day and birthday too!

Aldona Kairys
North Providence, RI

God's Point of View

This thing of getting older, many view as depletion,
However it's the one thing we're all going to do.
Although you may choose to view it as completion,
Nevertheless this all depends on your point of view.
Knowing your cup is not filled up to the brim,
Should you view this as half empty, or half full?
Gladly take time each day, to step back from the din,
Indulging in getting older from God's point of view.
Viewing the many great years now in our past,
Imagine your life and all you've been through;
Now catching a glimpse of God's eternal cast,
Gracefully enjoying it from God's point of view.

2 So as we celebrate today and the days yet to come,
0 Whether they be many, or few,
1 We'll understand it when our best is done,
3 As we see life completed from God's point of view.

A true thankful heart comes,
When one more fully understands:
God's point of view.

Elwood R. Buckwalter
Elizabethtown, PA

As I wrote this poem for Thanksgiving 2013, it became much more than just another Thanksgiving poem. I always believed in an almighty God who had a plan for everything in my life, but the concept of everything I just had to see it from God's point of view. As I went searching I discovered that even in my years of writing He was always revealing His point of view. Remember the two thieves crucified with Christ: they both saw His point of view but their choice determined their destiny and everyone has that same choice.

Without Freedom

In a beautiful cage
A colorful bird lives
The sight that he projects
Is very agreeable

A golden cage
Decorated with brilliant stones
Makes attractive the place

The beautiful bird
Fly side to side
To a reduced space
Keeps on with his goal
Of delighting us with his presence
And our hearts rejoice
With his songs

The satisfaction for us is complete
But…

Have we asked at any time
How is this innocent bird feeling
That has given up his freedom?

In addition to living alone,
He cannot give free reign to his wings
That he has in his body
To fly with liberty!

Nieves T. Nouel
Boca Raton, FL

He

He is absent
the talk with himself or with somebody
I don't know with whom…
Vo, Vo Vo… I want talk with him
No answer…
He come back
He is my life
When he is absent
I died

Bogda Tien
Coronado, CA

Farewell to My Poet-Friend

(In memory of the soul of Phan-Tan-My)

Oh, my poet-friend! Taking leave of this world
You are no longer entangled in the debt of nature
No more is there for you a busy complicated earthly existence
Your soul freely enters the leisurely fairyland
No longer surrounded by mankind's pleasures and grievances
Immediately you end your human sentimental troubles
You are in the blissful noble court of Heaven,
Your peaceful real native country for eternity…

Minh-Vien Nguyen
San Francisco, CA

Precious Love

Lost in this *precious love* I often cherish times like these,
I am so happy with you because it is also a time I can truly lay aside
Lost in this *precious love* are the cares and the worries of the day and
    all I can say is, *Please!*
I am full of energy because of each moment that I spend with you
    and rest at eventide

I often wonder as I sit alone and meditate
I think about positive things while twilight shadows fall
Birds are singing cheerful songs that I can relate
Earth stood still as sweet peace lies over us all

It is quite a pleasant day as fireflies begin to glow
Lost in this *precious love* in meadows all around;
Rain is starting to fall and a patchy mist is what there is to show
What a sight to see as it is close to the precious love *that I have found*

Dalston Harrison Jr.
Brooklyn, NY

Wishes with Grandma

I wish I was a big black bear
Bigger than anyone anywhere.

I wish I were a *doe*, seeking refuge in the forest I know.

If I was a fawn, I'd get up at dawn
And chew your beautiful manicured lawn.

I wish I was a kangaroo,
I'd make room in my pouch to carry two.

If I were king with a beautiful lion's mane,
No others strong as me, I'd put them all to shame!

I wish I was an *octopus*, with oh, so many arms
I'd surely be admired for my extra special charms.

If I were a *sea lion*, living in a pool,
Especially when it gets too hot,
I'd always feel so cool.

I wish I was a *zebra* with stripes all over me.
I'd run across the landscape, foot and fancy free.

Grandkids enjoy the rhymes, and please me when they laugh some.
I'm happy that my wish came true
They think their grandma's great fun.

Leatrice Bell
Wanaque, NJ

Defiance

They arrived in creaky wooden boats...

Anticipating a distant dream,
Multitude of disenchanted souls,
Enthusiastic in their pursuit,
Revolutionary thoughts...
Independence is a human birthright!
Courageous battles fought,
Accomplishments were many

Forming
A country that is concept...
Pride,
Guidance,
Loyalty,
Co-operation,
Freedom!

A land of diverse nations
Becoming one...
We are America!

Lynette
Philadelphia, PA

I began writing poetry at age fourteen. I was on the editorial staff of the high school literary magazine and was a contributor to the college literary periodical. I won second prize in a VFW script writing contest in 1976 and 1977. My first poem was published in the College Poetry Review *in spring 1982. In the summer of 1985, I entered the spoken word art scene; I found my niche with a group called the Philadelphia Poetry Forum. I have been published in the Poetry Forum Anthology and am a regular contributor to a newspaper in Venice Beach, California.*

Beauty Rest

The blue water waves, "Come to me"…
As far back as I can see.
Its peace and beauty,
Begin to soak into my weary city bones.

Seagulls, their low and melodic beat of wings,
Correlate the music of the waves.
Whitecaps dance and pirouette
For my eyes a scene I shan't forget.

I see in memory, large ships.
Their barges hauling us to them.
Masts high and proud,
They steam on by my memory's eye.

White peaks of sails, scattered about,
Their masters happily en route,
To nowhere soon
They're resting too — spirits renewed.

Small children play and gather stones
All colors, sizes, to take home,
Lovers love — and man and dog play, unaware
They're not alone.

O beautiful lake
You are a salve, to my soul.

Eva Ness
Pleasant Prairie, WI

I chose Lake Michigan as the setting because Kenosha is most known by it, and we that live here are prone to stay because of Lake Michigan. It is beautiful, God given natural beauty, and gives us coolness, serenity, peace and protection from storms. It is free entertainment and inspiration. When we first moved here in 1967, I loved to watch the huge ships slowly but surely cutting in and out and dreamily go by, seagulls calling out to one another, and the smell and quiet it offered. I hope I captured some of these feelings in my poems.

Climate Swindle

Science said in 1980, that there would be an
Ice Age and the results were zip,

Science said in 1985, that global cooling would
cause a world war concerning weather,

Science said in 1990, that raising sea level
would cause entire nations to disappear,

Science said in 1995, that rain forest should
be protected so civilizations could be saved,

Science said in 2000, that the Himalayan
glaciers would be gone in ten years,

Science said in 2005, that snow accumulation
would be a thing of the past,

Science said in 2010, that rain forests should
be saved or civilization could disappear,

Science said in 2015, that the arctic would
be ice free and ice increased,

Science said in 2020, that the science is
settled because the temperature also
increased one point two degrees in the world

Ronald L. Libengood
Colorado Springs, CO

Remember the Magic

Gone are the places where I used to play
Kingdoms found when out exploring one day
Replaced now by shadow streets, cold and strange
Hard to say when the world made this exchange

It's hard, but I think I remember that glow
That kids get with a secret that only they know
I've forgotten just how to make this joy last
And recover the wonder once felt in my past

It escapes in a giggle, or shines out in a grin
Children bursting with magic found only within
I feel it there in the back of my mind
Those fantasy kingdoms that I used to find

"Come dance and remember!" whispers the sun
The soft grass reminds me to laugh and have fun
Relief comes with knowing I'm not yet too old
If I try, these faded streets do not look so cold

How I love seeing things through the eyes of a child
To be able to love all things bright and wild
Times will come where I feel too old to play
So I'll remember the magic… at least for today!

Amy Pratt
Marion, IA

Last Glance

We begin the day
Somewhere in between
Dreams and sunrise,
The day grows and darkness fades,
Slipping, sliding, almost
Invisibly away—
Your last words,
Not from your voice,
But from your eyes,
Tell me you're
Still far away—
A traveler who's
Left me in that somewhere in between,
Behind,
And I am wondering,
If what they say
About winter's passing,
And the coming spring storms,
Is in that somewhere in between
Horizon's roaring red new sunrise,
And the flashing last glance,
Still crawling slowly through me,
From your deep, green eyes.

G. L. Bass
Pleasant Prairie, WI

A Fine, Fine Man

Four sons and a daughter
He made and raised
The daughter died at three
Four sons still carry his name
A fine, fine man

A call of despair and hysteria
Comes from the mother
The sons and wives trek to find
The fine, fine man being eaten away
From a disease called cancer
Why dear Lord, why must he suffer
Is it because seventy-three years
Of his life were fairly happy
Most of these years, to be exact, fifty
Are yet happily married
I ask why must He suffer
Is it because we crucified
Your son Jesus Christ
Even though He asked you for our forgiveness
Is it something You cannot do
So we all must suffer
And this is the time
For this fine, fine man

Betty Shlepr
Melbourne, FL

Reflection

I look in the mirror; what do I see?
A friend or stranger staring back at me?
I know I have aged, but did I age well?
A look at my reflection may not tell.

The scars on my face tell a story fine
In spite of them, does contentment outshine?
Does my countenance with joy radiate,
The message of my lips substantiate?

What do others see when they look at me?
I hope it's Jesus in me they see.
He has guided each step along the way
And given me purpose in ev'ry day.

Joy E. Krumdiack
Bellingham, WA

I have been writing poetry since I was ten years old. I enjoy writing for people and also from my experiences. I am retired and so now I have plenty of time to devote to my writing. I live in Bellingham, WA, with my husband and two adult daughters.

Callin' for Rain

I'm tired of this weather,
It's rained every day,
I guess I don't mind tho'
'Cause the team is away.

Their path took them east,
To Lake County, then Fort Wayne.
That's too far to travel,
I'll stay home. Let it rain.

But today the clouds are fluffy,
And the sun's shining down,
To make it much sweeter,
The boys are back in town.

Tonight they must play quickly,
I guess I should explain,
That later this evening,
They're callin' for rain!

Joyce M. Wilkerson
Clinton, IA

I'm from the small town of Clinton, IA, and there's nothing much to do. However, we are lucky enough to have a baseball team, the Clinton Lumberkings. They are a LoA team affiliated with the Seattle Mariners. I love baseball, so I go to as many games as I can, be it at home or on the road. Over the years I've experienced so many exciting moments that I decided to try writing a book, short stories, poems, limericks, even some jokes, all about baseball. This poem is my latest installment.

The Clawing at the Tree

She left
Without a word,
Like a bird
That sees a cat.

She flew west, left her nest
And nestlings with empty, gaping mouths.
Bound by love, the father stayed
And doubly paid, forlorn and wretched.

All for escape,
Unbound and free,
Now, she, alone,
Self-serving and celebrating.

And yet the night so changed her plight;
As shadows fell, she clung alone…
On empty branch, with futile dreams
And troubled sleep,

She could not see
The gaping mouth,
And hungry eyes,
And clawing at the tree.

Kenneth Swan
Marion, IN

'Sperience

He's got 'sperience they say
He's become old and grey
He's traveled many a mile
He's wearing a grin and not a smile
He's not natty nor neat
He's got sneakers on his feet
He's been there done that
He's got moth holes in his hat
He's kind and sweet
He's the one girls loved to meet
He's loved them one and all
He's bent to their beck and call
He's picked and chose
He's selected none of those
He's been taken by one from the east
He's in love with her through famine or feast
He's seen in her rapture from on high
He's watched in agony the day she died
He's erected a stone so grandiose
He's placed it in the pines she loved the most
He's sitting on the porch in deep thought
He's remembering the joy that she brought
He's got'n old and grey
He's got 'sperience so they say
'Xpedite

Larry K. Thomas
Crockett, TX

Being seventy-eight and world traveled, I have seen and experienced much. As a boy, I played in Japanese planes in the jungles of the Philippines, climbed through German coastal fortifications on the coast of France, and lived with poor Korean mountain people on the DMZ. I lived with and for all those people. I married a Korean War orphan. She tolerated me for fifty years, what a woman, what love! At this stage you give away tailored suits, tux, tails, and settle into some worn jeans and shirt, sit on the porch and watch the sun go down — what a life!

Pennies Are Hard to Get

The first penny I ever had
I dropped on the outhouse floor.
It bounced and spun a couple times
then went through a crack beside the door.

I was three years old, and had been told
to keep my pennies in my pocket deep.
But on that day when it rolled away,
I learned that pennies are hard to keep.

Many days then passed by,
before I was given one more cent.
And when I was told to pinch it tight,
I knew exactly what they meant.

That penny came quite hard, back then.
To my loose tooth they tied a string,
then tied the string to the outhouse door
and slammed the stupid thing!

That penny, I earned the painful way,
when they slammed the outhouse door.
So I spent it on my fourth birthday
at the general store.

Thought I would do something special
on my fourth birthday,
so I made a down payment
on a nickel Milky Way.

Leeland Wilson
Evart, MI

I was born in 1932. This poem reflects one of my most outstanding memories of the Great Depression.

Homeward

I was born
To the sound of waters
The cadence of creeks
Starlight on the lakes
The singing of the surf
That wheeling, mewing of gulls
The wonder of viewing
Dolphins and flying fish
Cavorting in their natural playscape

And when I'm gone
Scatter my dreamings
Along the flowing river Huron
From the shores of Gittchi-Gommi
   Marigot Bay — Sitka Harbor
     Bahia Todos Los Santos
     The sands of Kam-kura
       And remember this
       Real love always lasts forever!

Donald Ransom
Detroit, MI

Things

Why do we cling
To what is a thing
When we actually know
That's all it can be?

Yet, when it's a gift,
From one who is special,
The thought behind it
Is what makes it actual.

The time will come
That we will be gone,
And all that we cherished
Will also be gone, but where?

Selma Gutierrez
Raton, NM

Gifts to Remember

If roses grow in Heaven, Lord,
Please pick a bunch for me…
Place them in my husband's arms,
A gift of beauty, for him to see…

Tell him that I love him
And miss him very much…
I reach for his empty pillow,
And give a gentle touch…

Remembering the good times
Going back "somewhat" in time…
I always worked with children,
While he was solving crimes…

The perfect gift he gave me
(Here's a little clue)
Is our wonderful children
Bringing pleasure through and through

Kristi Herring
Banning, CA

Scurry Up Scamps

The scurry up scamps of Merry-go-town
On the banks of the Dudley now wretched and brown
Never look up nor ever look down
They stare straight ahead going 'round and around
Passing time rushing hither thither and yon
While calliopes toodle the scurry up song

Merry go scurry go worry go 'round
The scurry up scamps of Merry-go-town

Young scamps go to school but still go around
Albeit in orbits that circle the town
They practice all day the scurry up song
'Til they never look up nor ever look down
Then Doctor Malarkey, profound of profound
Finds each scamp a future in Merry-go-town

Merry go scurry go worry go 'round
The scurry up scamps of Merry-go-town

Perfect made scamps though he called them nouns
He gave them a spaceship though nouns called it ground
But they never looked up when Perfect looked down
So he said of this race, "I shan't e'er be bound"
Hence they just travel around and around

Merry go scurry go worry go 'round
A scamp once looked up saw Perfect and frowned
And his tears dribble dibbled over the ground
Into the Dudley now wrenched and brown

Seth Richards
Lucerne, CA

My Best Friend

Tied and sitting all alone.
I took the steps to reach you.
Your light brown eyes filled with longing.
The need and want to be loved.
One day you became my best friend.
Fourteen years we shared.
And now my heart breaks with your loss.
Somehow I feel I let you down.
You were there for me but was I there for you?
I tried to protect you.
I tried to make you happy.
We did spend many happy times together.
But were they enough?
I saw your pain and heard your cries.
I felt it too—we shared each other's pain
It took all my strength.
I knew I needed to stop your pain.
To say goodbye and on that day
I saw it in your eyes.
You knew I understood.
It was as if you spoke and said,
Thank you Mommy, I love you.
My Jay J always in my heart!

Florence Compher
Wartburg, TN

Love's Destiny

Money comes — money goes, for me it did not matter
I loved you head to toes, even though our clothes were a tatter.
But your heart was untrue and your head led your way
My true heart turned a dark hue as you walked out that day.
The pain of loss pierced my heart, but life forced me forward
I wandered aimlessly through days with my heart mortared.
My life recycled and brought one who loves me dearly
Our hearts are encircled ringing with our love truly.
My past burned to ashes and my heart is again happy
My fortune returned and we have a bouncing baby.
Your head was ruthless and used to getting its own way
I observed your sadness as your heart shriveled more each day.
The last time I saw you, secrets in your face told of trouble
Your new life was untrue, I read about the burst of your bubble.
Remembering you as I put the paper down on the table
I wiped a tear from my eye with a wish it was a fable.

Elaine Carroll Kelley
Riverside, CA

Ashley

Just for a short moment
We are here!
I reflect on this
As down my face, runs a tear
I hurt for you, I hurt for me
My arms ache to hold you;
Hold you, as if you were my own
But little Ash, away you flew
You're at peace, Ashley; I am not
More than anything, you wanted love
I always knew that, Ash!
You have that now, up above
Ashley, with your dimples
And your impish grin
You are now loved unconditionally
In your world there is no sin
Smile down upon us
Let us know that it's okay
To release you, to let you go,
To continue our lives, to laugh and play
Good-bye my little Ash
Be the angel that you are
I'll be looking up above
For that one special star

Your friend,
Rhonda

Rhonda L. Redetzke
Bowman, ND

Let's Celebrate

July brings temperatures rising
As we celebrate this day
People having picnics
All across the USA
Lovers walking hand in hand
With passion in their eyes
Fireworks will soon explode
As we celebrate this July
Families drinking lemonade
From stands their children made
People sitting under trees
Trying to cool off in the shade
The water sparkles in the sun
Inviting all to swim
Lifeguards busy watching
For trouble that may begin
Sand castles line the beach
For the contest soon to start
The contestants are all anxious
For the judges to do their part
The memories that they'll make
Will last a lifetime through
Happy Independence Day
America God bless you

Cherie Chilvers
San Bernardino, CA

Dear Brother

Dear brother, who means the world to me,
I know you felt like nobody loved you.
It breaks my heart how you don't feel
a part of our family.
Everything you were told your whole
life was completely untrue.

Dear brother, it wasn't right how we
were robbed of special bonding time.
There's so many things I'd go back
and change if I could.
I'll never understand why you were
taken from us while in your prime.
All that I ask is for a sign that you're
happy now if you would.

Dear brother, I wear your ring close
to my heart.
I think about you everyday.
My sisterly love is so great death
can't even part.
Until I see you again, this I pray.

Abigail Hucker
Chester, PA

Such Love, Such Mercy

Sometimes, oftentimes feeling alone and yet
Never alone am I! Look my ever-changing feelings
In the eye, I tell them I will not yield to them,
I tell them to flee! Because of His great love, I can
Be strong, confident, and free!
Praying, reading, meditating, reflecting on His
Amazing love, His sweet and tender mercies,
His precious, abiding love…
Knowing confidently He has given me a life filled
With joy abundantly; and though testing and trials will
Not cease, because I know what His word says,
I hope and put my trust in His Son given for me.
I stand in awe in one so magnificent, so holy.
I stand in awe knowing it is through Him only.
In divine love, sacrificed for me, I reflect and ponder what
Tender mercy, amazing grace, and joy I now have in spite
Of the trials I face! Because of His redeeming love shown
In the sacrificial death of His Son, I am now made clean, holy!
I can now call upon Him, my One and only everlasting God.
As I ponder His great love, how He knew me before
There was even a me, and despite me and all of my sin,
He continues to love me because I have chosen to believe
In Him who died for me, and accept Him as my Lord and Savior!
Such amazing love! Such sweet, tender mercies!
I stand in awe of God's love and everlasting favor…

Michelle Lynn Anderson
Locust Grove, VA

Alone Again

Well, it happened to me again, Lord
After I gave it my all
Held out for just so long
Then—oops, I let myself fall
I listened to the sweet talk
Believed it all like before
Then all that love took a walk
Without warning, went right out the door
Wish I knew how it can change so fast
In love today—out of love tomorrow
Even though I've seen it in the past
Still, it always leaves much sorrow
Each time I tell myself "no"
When someone new comes along
Then when I let my heart go
That's when I hear "so long"
The slow eating hurt inside
When he no longer makes a call
Trying to smile on the outside
Like it really doesn't matter at all
But it does when you really care
Like I always seem to do
Being so happy when he wanted me there
Enjoying a great life for two
The same thoughts go through my mind
Lord, where did I go wrong?

Daisyann Fredericks
Canajoharie, NY

Of Whiskey Rye and Cuban Cigars

Smoke, swirls first then rises.
Cuban cigar, 'tween fingers liberating.
Air and smoke from deep within, exhaled,
adding to its likeness swirling, rising.
Out here, atop a white bench I sit,
upon my front porch seat, watching, waiting.

As shadows lengthen, begins soft breezes to whisper
in the face of oncoming sunset. I reach
for my glass, crystal, rye whiskey filled
and upon tongue and pallet I swirl. With
eyes closed, I savor its taste, rough and raw edged.

The sky dims, dusk approaches, yet not quite reached.
Spring, its green earth embraces the lingering
warmth of this day. I grasp my glass, swirl
its contents, sipping the rawness. Within it slides,
while outside, shadows deepen; dusk settles in.

Oblivion, this day's, draws near. 'Tween lips placed
the Cuban, another drag is taken; its essence inhaled,
deep within my marrow. I hold it there, allowing
alcohol, nicotine and human physiology to mix;
permeating surrounding cells, altering euphorically
thoughts of my life's hardened margins slowly
succumbing to its last day's final dawning.

Hugo T. William
Eugene, OR

Dangerous Kiss

Driving along Skagit City Road early on a sunny Saturday
morning, the world was alive with late February gladness,

green plants in the fields had already broken the muddy
surface with their linear look, small gaggles of trumpeter

swans were digging their bills deep for food, crooking their
long necks, and waddling along, paying little attention

to the trumpeters leading the way. Red-tailed hawks
and white-headed eagles positioned on bare-limbed trees

above the road, kept track of the proceedings as fleets
of low-flying birds, dark and fast, swooped and swirled

over the meadows in perfect syncopation, stopping now
and then to rest and feed. Taken in by nature's lively

drama, the couple stashed their car in the church parking lot
and headed for the dike and an elevated view of the action.

As they walked across the road, the young woman suddenly
turned and embraced the older guy, the two of them in a

prolonged kiss, standing on the double yellow line. When
they returned to their senses, they expected to see cars in both

lanes, the drivers smiling, waiting for them to move. Instead,
there was nothing but a faint sense of the church's clapboard

presence, the distant sounds of the swans trumpeting their glee
and, perched in a nearby tree high above, the steady gaze

of a lone eagle, looking intently at the scene below, wondering,
perhaps, if there was something to prey about.

Robert Skeele
LaConner, WA

For Mother

When I look back at the years I grew up,
Many memories seem to come to mind.
Birthday cakes you made,
John's were checkerboards,
Chocolate were mine.

A birthday party on a cold January day,
I wondered where the Anderson twins had been.
They were at my house with others yelling,
"Surprise!" when I walked in.

The 1939 Ford trips to California,
Each summer, we would go.
And all the clothes you made for me,
With such talent, you would sew.
We said goodbye just a few years ago,
And, I hope you somehow know,
You always will be remembered,
We all love you so!

Nan Tebrinke
Red Oak, IA

Praise

With this world in such disarray,
    I think it is time we let God have His say.
We need to stop, look and listen.
    For only then can we see His works glisten.
The sun shining bright.
    The moon glowing in the night.
The stars up in the sky.
    Even the breath we need to sigh.
Children laughing with such delight.
    The snow sparkling ever so white.
His heart listening each time we pray.
    The enemy He helps us hold at bay.
The farmland with the richest soil ever seen.
    The vegetables we grow, fit for a queen.
From the clothes we wear on our back,
    To the groceries we carry in a sack.
The house we live in.
    All the "things" that have been.
The games we play to win.
    Every day living when we sin.
God provides all, in this life, as we live.
    He only asks us to ask Him to forgive.
And now it is time, as a minister once said, to
    "Each in your own words. Each in your own way,
For a world united in peace, bow your head and pray."

Margaret Jackie Breker
North Vernon, IN

The Loafer

I don't care if anyone else is upset or wroth,
I'm happy being a lazy sloth.
Doing housework and chores I'll often postpone,
but I don't care, I live by myself, and I'm on my own.
I like to sit on my couch, in my pajamas, and watch TV, and eating
   junk food, and what do I care?
As long as I'm clean and shaved, and I've combed my hair.
I like to lay in my hammock on summer afternoons in the warm
   shiny sun,
accomplishing very little, and leaving things undone.
In the mind of many, and perhaps in the eyes of some,
I look like a thoughtless careless irresponsible bum.
But, my personal lifestyle I really don't have to apologize for
   or excuse.
I'm free to live the life I choose.
None of us is perfect we all have a flaw,
I know I have faults, but then don't we all?
I'll live this way till the day I die, though my life may appear
   strange or even odd.
But I'm still a worthwhile person, a human being, in the mind and
   eyes of God.

Alan Knight
Champaign, IL

*During the summer, when it's hot and humid, I feel slow and lethargic. I really
don't feel like doing much. So I felt inspired to write a poem about not doing much
during the summer season.*

The Memory of You

As a gentle
sunbeam
on a clear summer afternoon,
your memory
illuminates my days —
deeply etched in the pattern
of my soul.

María del Carmen Rodríguez
North Brunswick, NJ

María del Carmen Rodríguez is a counselor, educator and consultant. Since early childhood, she has been attracted to all the arts. Her mother taught her music appreciation, wise faith and love of family, and her father instilled in her a deep respect for nature and community. She is the proud mother of a college graduate who embodies grace and peace. She uses the arts in her training of new counselors who are empowered to facilitate clients' holistic healing. She has trained counselors for twenty-five years and her research includes bereavement after a neonate loss and folk-healers' role in spirituality-oriented counseling.

Portrait of a Bully

Humble beginnings you had, in ocean waves,
Obscure, unassuming, hardly were you noticed.
Though baby steps you took brought you raves,
Accolades, trophies, weren't on you lavished.

Wandering without aim, skimming the surface,
No one saw greatness, purpose or gain.
Another wasted soul, sure to fail and disgrace,
Like school dropouts and society's pain.

You defied the odds, you grew and grew.
Gathering strength, now you were noticed.
Folks from lands afar now laid eyes on you;
Soon envy, and then fear, you instilled.

Your fury and destruction will soon abate,
When land you encounter ends your run.
Tornadoes and floods you unleash come late,
For nature's fury begins to soon wane.

When storms clear and your death you meet,
Will you find within your heart and your soul,
Any remorse; and forgiveness do you seek?
Or to your grave, without guilt, you gladly crawl?

Or is there a mission to your life, after all?
Were you nature's way to distill and carry
Water precious, to many a distant landfall?
So, purposeful was even the bluster and fury?

Is this the reason why you've been christened,
Sanitized names like Sandy, Allen and Katrina?

Puthalath K. Raghuprasad
Odessa, TX

Old Man Time

Old man time carries the years
With a heavy sigh,
Weighed down by the chains of time
He drags them on until we die,
The months, years go by; old
Man time kept track because he
Doesn't lie,
A faithful record of time's passage
On earth he keeps,
Until we return to dust;
In eternal rest sleep.

Robert A. Calhoun
Philadelphia, PA

Wonderland

I wonder what Wonderland would be,
If Sour Patch monkeys hung in a tree.
If raindrops were gum drops they would fall from the sky,
Cotton candy roller coasters would go way up high.
If Skittles were rainbows, so bright and so bold,
At the end of the rainbow there would be candy wrappers of gold.
If candles were candy corn they would shine lots of light,
Hershey bars would turn into s'mores at the end of the night.

Avery Morgan
South Park, PA

Nature Made

A white bridal veil blows with the south breeze,
Designed and completed on top of a juniper bush.
Completed by a patient spider, it's beautiful as you please.
Transferred to bride's shining hair and held with a pin.
A glowing bride of small stature, she will take her vows
At the side of her groom in front of their preacher.
The vows made together to love, and care for each other,
So strong to have lasted fifty-six years.
Memories linger,
Tough decisions made together with her work as a teacher,
His work as a factory supervisor and farm owner.
They had a family and stayed true to each other, no fears.
Now that he left for Heaven, she holds his memory close.
Each day she looks at the family picture, she says a prayer.
Before turning off the light at night, she turns in the bed where
They slept so many years, shuts her eyes to sleep.
She is proud, staying true to the vows
Made so very long ago. Memories recalled, by viewing a
Spider nature made white bridal veil.

In loving memory of her husband, Jim, in June 2015,
One year following his journey
From Earth to Heaven.

Bonnie Neuman
Evart, MI

I am a retired art educator and one of the founder's of our OLAH (Osceola League of Arts and Humanities). We have a building for selling art and antiques. I volunteer there.

The Seed of Love

A seed is such a tiny thing
But oh how powerful
Inside its shell awaiting still
Longing, longing, to reveal

Its patience has no limits
It tires not a day
Knowing that its time will come
When soil and sunshine have their way

Planted in the proper clime
It then will come alive
Sprouting forth a lively growth
Abundance for mankind

God the Father waited long
To plant His "seed" of love
By Holy Spirit pure and good
Through Mary, then brought forth her son

Through Jesus we can now "come forth"
The "planted" seed of God
In soil and sunshine of His grace
Bringing forth to others this "seed of love"

Doris Applegate
Harlan, IN

This "seed of love" was planted in my life at age twelve. At eighty-four years I still try to show forth the love of God to others. What a wonderful life I have!

WWIII—911

As I watch World War III unfold
I'm sure there's much left untold,
Nine-one-one takes on new meaning today
As terrorists seem to have their way.
My neighbor called me on the phone,
She didn't want to be alone.
It's an eerie feeling to go outside,
And not see a single plane in the sky.
The terrorists made a big mistake,
The American people they underestimate.
People covered in soot and perspiration,
As they tear and dig with desperation,
Trying to save one more life,
Someone's daddy or someone's wife.
It breaks my heart to see on TV
Arabic children, celebrating victory.
Looking at the destruction and rubble,
Anyone can see the world's in serious trouble.
If the terrorists want a fight,
America will the world unite.

Dianne Mulcahy
High Springs, FL

The New Beginning

He/she has crossed over,
Gone on to a better place;
At least that's the way we console each other
When someone passes away.
Then we paint pictures of Heaven,
God's paradise in the sky,
We don't think of the possibility
That it might be a big lie…
For "being born again" is the key;
It's offered to each individual soul,
And from the beginning of your birth
God put you in control.
And we who remain can only hope
That the gift of God was received
For it's only "the new beginning"
To those who accepted and believed.

Robert E. Brock
Hampton, VA

Sal's Song

We sat at a table and waited to hear,
Reminisce, sing the songs that we hold so dear.
DJ Nick introduced them to the crowd
As we all applauded and cheered real loud.

When the music began we got up to dance.
Some songs were fast, some told of romance.
We listened, remembered and sang along,
Those old, old memories returned so strong.

Then Sal got up and walked to the mike.
He's a friend of ours that we really like.
He was dedicating the next song to his wife —
His partner, his sweetheart, the love of his life.

The name of the song was "I Believe"
Since current life issues caused them to grieve.
He sang to Mary, and we all could feel
That his caring and tenderness were so very real.

As he sang the song, no eyes remained dry.
We couldn't stop crying, no matter how hard we tried.
A very special moment that we all got to share
With Sal, Mary and all who were there.

Anita Tornow
West Milford, NJ

Sal and Mary suffered the loss of their daughter, their only child, in an auto accident. In addition to them, she left behind two teenage daughters and her husband. Sal came to the bank one day and I showed him a poem I wrote about a fellow worker. He looked at me with a look of sadness on his face and asked if I could write a poem about him. I thought back to the night when I went to see him sing with some of my friends and knew that would be the subject of my poem.

How Do I Look to You

When I was twenty, I was looking nice…
I'm a girl… had to be the sugar and spice!

When I was thirty and so much more…
I didn't know what I was looking for!

Some now say I look like forty-something…
That's what living a good life can bring!

Others do say I look over fifty…
Those are the days I'm looking spiffy!

Actually, I am proud to be sixty-plus…
So tell me, can I have a seat on the bus?

Seventy, eighty and ninety too…
I look forward to looking at you!

One hundred years plus the twenty…
My life will be complete… good and plenty!

Saundra Russell
Tucson, AZ

A Spectral Heart

Hark!
The violin's aching sobs
Sing of glory long since faded
In sweetness, and agony

Such like my foolish heart
To grasp those fleeting, spectral notes
In a quest for grace
Amidst decay

Rachelle Fried
King of Prussia, PA

Friendly Guys

Little bumblebee buzzing around,
You make such a humming sound.
Gold and black with furry body,
You also have a very fat belly.
I watch you sipping nectar among my shrubs and flowers.
You can be seen hovering for hours and hours.
Busy as a bee is not just a cute saying
For these are not games you are seen playing.
What we would do without you it is hard to say,
I truly hope you furry "can't fly" guys are indeed, here to stay.

Linda R. Dreyer
Cumberland, WI

Father's Day

Da Da who taught me how to walk and talk.
Changing my diapers? Probably not.
Pop who taught me right from wrong.
To the radio singing the same old song.
And always making me feel like I belong.
Dad tried to teach me something he liked I might enjoy
…football, fishing or that big boy toy.
So bad did I feel no joy in any to be had;
I look back now and feel so sad.
Father a hero a friend: working hard to make meat's end.
Tell him to slow down; don't even bother.
Hard at work or play it just didn't matter.
A tear rolls from my eye,
wondering why did he have to die.
You left this world way too soon,
the noon of your life.
Feeling the gloom of it all cuts me like a knife.
I hope you're up there playing with new wonders.
"Gadget Willy" making more blunders and acting all silly.
Casting your line in the sea of tranquility,
hoping for that big one,
be it fish or jackpot winning.
Never got to tell you I loved you from the beginning.

Robert J. Vogt
Schenectady, NY

First and foremost I am a very creative person able to be creative with almost anything I put my mind to. If it's writing, drawing, photography, or inventing I love to think outside the box. As an artist with a graphic design degree, I enjoy drawing strange things being my first passion if not profession. I'm afraid I view writing and photography as mere hobbies even if I might have missed my calling; I always received As in my creative writing college classes but only Cs in my drawing classes. In poetry, my influences would be Dr. Seuss and Edgar Allan Poe. I believe poems should tell a story or give an opinion. I personally also believe that poems should rhyme, or what's the point? "Father's Day" is a poem dedicated to my father who passed away on February 9, 2014. I tried to make it a more generic poem but it quickly became much more personal.

The Ruler

I remember way back yonder
When yardsticks were free
Merchants put their advertisements
On them for us to see

It was always handy
To measure anything
It could measure snow in winter
Or rain when it came

It was made from a tree
That grew for you and me
It seemed to be needed
In every home to be

It could be the rod of discipline
For the training of a child
It could stand in the corner
Ready for time of trial

It could measure the highness of a child
To put a mark on the wall
To show a record of our growth
As we stretched to be tall

It has been called a ruler
But a ruler it can't be
Because when it does its work
It must depend on me

Omar A. Walker
Bluejacket, OK

Sorrow's Path

The loss of a loved one is the most personal
Profound agony one endures
Death is a reality, an end that we are assured

The idea of never being able to see, touch or talk
To one another again is crushing
Is this selfishness—yes? Tears of lost, you're lost,
Your pain comes rushing

You are the one deprived of their love, friendship,
And their tender touches and words
Others speak how sorry but in your darkness
Their remarks go unheard

As the hours, days, months pass, once again
You feel their loving presence lingering near
Then you realize how lucky and blessed you have been

It is worth the pain to have known the love of a lover,
Child, parent, best friend
Our faith and memories help heal our grief
Until the time when we meet again

Marie D. Raymond
Sheldon, VT

For My Pixie

The first poem I wrote, three years ago, was "My Three
Little Dogs,"
And now I must write about my tale of woe.
This April past, I lost my Yorkie, Pixie,
And she's missed by me and her sisters, Dixie and Trixie.
I still see her showing me the paw and making her noises,
While being stubborn and showing her poses.
I still feel her with me when holding her sisters,
It's hard to explain how much I miss her.
Pixie succumbed to cancer after an eight-month length,
She was only nine years old but too weak to keep up her strength.
The last day she lived I saw her try,
To not give up and stay by my side.
I saw her tell here sisters and friends,
Don't be worried, I know my life is at an end.
She looked at me as if to say,
Goodbye Mommy I'll see you another day.
I know she went to Heaven as all dogs should,
She's in my heart as no other dog could.
I feel her love and see her face in my dreams,
And someday soon only memories will remain.
But I'll never forget her wonderful years,
If this page is wet, it's only my tears.
Thank you Pixie and your *sweet little face,*
For being part of my life and for loving me!

Marie L. Paris
Edgewater, FL

My first poem, "My Three Little Dogs," was published on page fifty-one of This
Time Around: Voyage, *Eber & Wein Publishing, in 2013. Of all the dogs in
my life, Pixie stood out the most with her diva attitude, funny tricks, and love of
life. I felt a need to write a poem dedicated to her and found out, by doing so, it
helped me to see how sweet she was and how much I loved her. Anyone who ever had
a dog like her would understand how lucky they were to have them in their life.*

In Memory of a Star

I know that I have dented if not broken a heart or two in my time
And mine has felt the pain of love refused or spurned in my time too.
The former some may say was simply selfishness and what was there
The latter we who've been there may chalk it up as just deserts.
There was a star, though, a movie star, whose films
Would leave me spellbound. It was her eyes,
Her beauty too but in her eyes a longing to be loved.
A film of hers I'd never miss and watching her I'd think,
Poor girl, here too she still seeks love—it's in her eyes—
And this is but a movie.
And to be in movies was never my ambition. The part I dreamed of
Was in her life where I might have given her the love she longer for
But now she's dead and suicide they say.
For lack of love did she take her life?
And leave me with her picture on my coffee mug?

Peyton Chamberlain Jr.
Georgetown, TX

*What's not important is the person, me. What is important is what the person
does, which would be nothing without the gift of life, from whence, from what, from
whom—who knows—but like all gifts the recipient owes not only thanks but
something in return. Like the gift of talent, one is expected to make use of it. I have
the gift of life and talent both. Something, somehow, somewhere, which freely uses
nature to get its way, wants me to continue writing and has nudged me to poetry.*

Pipe-Free Santa Never for the
Children and Adults Who Believe

While listening to a good joke
Santa loves to smoke
Wearing his Santa Claus cap
While wee folks
Wait their turn
To sit on Santa's lap

While some elves are busy
Feeding the reindeers
For the long journey
The other elves
Fill the sleigh with toys
For all the good girls and boys

The reindeers are waiting
For Santa to eat his snack
He will light his pipe
Only when he is relax
Santa Claus will show
The reindeers know
For the long haul overnight

Therese Jacques Gamache
Chepachet, RI

What inspired me to write this poem is what I read on the Call Newspaper *about an anti-smoking woman from the New England states. She wanted a smoke-free Santa.*

Manifold Blessings

Faithfully bestowed upon us by our God,
Mercy and strength for the path we trod.
Out of His endless storehouse above
He showers blessings from His heart of love.
His limitless power He wants to show
On our journey to Heaven, as we walk here below.
Riches untold are poured out through His grace
As we kneel in His presence and look in His face.
The rough is made smooth, the bitter made sweet
As we lay them before His nail-scarred feet.
Learn to trust and believe Him, whatever your lot
For He always comes through in the toughest spot.
Look to His promises, put Him to the test
And you'll find that He always brings what is best!

Margaret R. Smith
Hobe Sound, FL

A Wistful Journey

On a cool and faded November afternoon,
I returned to the town of my Peter Pan days
and there found much was still the same
yet so much more had been so very changed.
The dense, mighty forest behind our old house,
where as a boy I romped and hollered,
laughed and ran and played,
had been conquered by developers
and subjugated into a subdivision stain.
The school buildings, which once encased
my early years of childhood learning
and all those friends, loves and daydreams chased,
have since been ripped down,
leaving vacant lots to take their place.
I strolled down along Main Street
glad to see that Time had made no real claim
and yet saddened was I to find
not one familiar face
nor any voice to call my name.
Finally my wistful journey took me
to the graveyard where long ago friends
and I dared each other in Halloween games.
There among the ancient mossy stones
the wind with a haunted whisper did proclaim,
"Remember. Remember.
For 'tis only us here who remain."

M. K. Frederick
Cincinnati, OH

M. K. Frederick lives in Cincinnati. He began writing at the age of sixteen and has continued with it for the last thirty-five years. The inspiration for this poem came in the fall of 2014, when news of his old high school being torn down prompted the author to return to the small town of his youth. On this tour of old familiar haunts, he discovered that not only was the high school gone along with many other places, but more profoundly, the realization that he had become a complete stranger in a town he once called home.

Cyclic Wonders

Rain it comes and then it goes, where it goes no one knows.
Out comes sun to sprinkle joy.
Just as quick the sun is gone chased away with wintry bubbles.
Wind returns blustering away glistering dewy night's air.
Darkness shades its nightly wonder watching in stillness
As glowing worms a wiggle and wiggle sliding on fields
Mixed now with dewy dewdrops petals.
Watching when the glow returns, as cycle comes and yes it goes.
Quick as night foxes jump the tall grasses chasing bunnies
   grazing slow.
Spring has sprung the sun is here again; then clasped a thunder
   shades in grey
Singles out tsar's night's array day's agenda
Slows too wonder bringing in the summer's slumber.
Clouds whisper nightly scenes, surrendering into paleness.
As night's agenda leaves us all aghast!

Carol Lynn Swenson
Eustace, TX

God's Special Creations

I have four zebra finch.
They are very special…
Two came to me
For my eighty-first birthday…
I named them Dum and Dee.
Later three babies were born…
Two girls and a boy…
I kept Love and gave
Faith and Hope away…
Soon I had another boy — Joy.
I put the two brothers in a cage.
After some time they were fighting.
I traded Joy for a girl…
I got my Faith back…
I had a heart attack.
Birds were lost without me…
I love *my birds*, so much…
I ask the boys, "How are you?"
They kiss their mates…
This is a sign they love me, too.
"I am loved."
I was gone four days.
I missed them terribly…
Now I'm back and taking over again,
Wondering how I could live without them.

Eleanor A. Tingelstad
Fergus Falls, MN

I had a heart attack and survived! God didn't want me in Heaven yet. He told me, "Go back home and write some more poetry." So here's one for you about my most precious possessions: my birds. Sure enough there was a letter in my mailbox asking for a new poem.

Yearning Reflections

You see the moon, and the moon sees me,
I'd love to be where you want to be
However the distance, no matter how far,
Even if up to that bright shiny star
You gaze at it from there, and I still see it too,
As always with me, and always with you.
But years have come and gone,
Time floating through our days,
Our lives so far apart now, and
Swished so far away, but whenever that
Old moon shines down, I still think you see it too,
Connecting threads that shone silver then, but now
Contain a shade of blue. But, whenever I do think
Of you, those yearnings still in part—
Will forever reflect that big old moon
That connects you to my heart.

Carol E. Gange
Baltimore, MD

I'm retired now, after thirty years as a construction company office manager.
This is my tenth published poem, and as usual it contains words to do with
love and romantic interjections. Love is such a strong emotion and makes life
worthwhile. But just as essential is the imagination in expressing and creating
beautiful poetry that can touch a heart with tender, fulfilling passion, that may
bring a gentle tear to one's eye and sentiment through the heartstrings of our
existence. I'm thankful for this opportunity to create.

God's Pretty Picture

And now! ...in Charleston, at that
    black church
'mid Bible study, song and chat
    a lurch...!

O' nine! ...you went to sleep that Wednesday night
but not at home or in your bed —
for 'neath a mask of fleece snow-white
a wolf! ...And you the prey that bled
    to death.

Again a boat is rocked! Waves give birth to Fear!
Again a voice commands, "Peace! ...Be still."
And from a cross, one word He'd have us hear:
"Forgive." A net is cast... and His to fill.

"As a mother comforts her child, I
will comfort you." With doubt erased, you can believe
your ears... "Sh–hhh, come here... look up and dry
your eyes... and blow your nose... oh, use your sleeve!"

And Paul in Athens offered his "bread."
Hooves and heels halting... hushing.
"...some of your own poets have said
we are His offspring..."

A pretty picture God had seen
and ere we came He'd saved a place —
'mid colors black and white, and shades between
where we could shine... His face.

    An eye blinks: nine crowns! Alike.

Carrie M. Grindley
Oakwood, IL

A Special Time

It's time to live a different kind of life
A life that contains no strife.
Lazy mornings, late lunches and late nights
I'm taking life to new heights.
No starting time, no quitting time
It's about time!
No schedules, only rest and relaxation.
Savoring every moment of this wonderful vacation.
Want to rest, relax and rejuvenate
So much to see and to do — can't wait!
Taking time to enjoy the harvest
This has to be life at its best.
Now's the time to get to work
Working hard, that is, at enjoying
Each and every perk.
What is this wonderful time, life's main event,
Why it's my retirement!
Can't wait to embrace it, live it and love it
Making new memories that I can covet.
It's been a long time coming
Listen to me I'm humming!
I look forward to this adventure of mine
Living it a day at a time!

Fran Hvidsten
Staten Island, NY

I've been happily married for twenty-five years. We've been retired for six years and love having the freedom retirement brings: getting to spend time together and doing things that interest us. We have five children and are blessed with seventeen grandchildren. I love being home, cooking, reading books, doing crossword puzzles and trying my luck at the casinos. I love game shows and a good movie. My poem was created before I retired when reflecting on what retirement would bring. I am at a great time in my life and enjoy every moment of it. I feel truly blessed!

Somehow... I Like It!

What fools these mortals be!
It's enough to make you take to sea.

Even as God's love shines everything into existence
Ignorance has a way of having a persistence
And you can meet it with indifference or resistance.

Best to swim in a clear water lake
And let the cosmic powers do their bake —
But evolution is not a piece of cake!

Are we flotsam in the stream of a living dream?
Are we plankton interrupting the inner sanctum?
Are we puff pastry on the shelf of life
Thrown into a world of strife,
Marching to the tune of an unseen drummer
As the pendulum of justice swings like a scythe!

Could we be puppets in a Punch and Judy show
Contained in a background cosmic glow —
Or are we spirits with bodies coming to and through!

But remember — the wearer of the coat is not the coat
But the captain of the boat
Who remains afloat
And I could file a complaint — but I won't!

Because — somehow... I like it!

Henry F. Mende
New City, NY

The inspiration for this poem, "Somehow... I Like It!," was born from an undying optimism that all trials and tribulations can be overcome with love, which can also contribute to an enhanced sense of humor. Indeed some people have seen me as a "Pollyanna optimist," outrageously out of whack with reality like a man falling off a cliff in the full lotus position while reading the Bhagavad Gita — but so what! The point in my mind is that we are here in "the sport of the infinite" and we just haven't quite caught up to that fact yet.

Loneliness

I know you, oh so well
You have been my companion for so long
I believe you plan to stay a spell.

I look at you and then I think
If I'll just get up and leave
Maybe you will go away
But as soon as I return
I find your back to stay

I wonder if people really know
What awful pain you bring
Or if they even notice
That I hardly ever sing

You've stolen my joy, my peace, my life
And left me sad at heart
I know I need to let you go
I just don't know how to start

Maybe one day very soon
Someone will stop long enough to see
That just a visit or a call
Would drive you away from me

My heart would dance, my spirit sore
If just once in a while
Someone would stop by
And knock on my front door

Helon Phillips
Cordesville, SC

A Love Sonnet to My Beautiful Wife, Ethel

I'm so sorry you're in the hospital,
You're my best friend and pal,
I'm listening to a song by Bryan Adams
Called "Heaven"
When we're together,
That's where I am.

You won't be in the hospital forever,
Only forever is forever,
Our love is forever,
It is never never,
I love you so
From head to toe.

When I'm alone, I'm sad,
When we're together I'm glad.

Alfred Elkins
Bronx, NY

Bixby

By and by I think of him
His poetry: some solemn and grim
As for all his loss: rightly so
And cause of his woe
He talks of his daughter 'neath the sodden grass
Oh how he missed the young lass
Yet he did still hold
A sense of humor with the stories he told
His wife whose knitting, somehow was never finished
Or how his looks over time, slowly diminished
Tales of life, politics and war
So many tears he shed and pain his heart bore
He kept on writing through the years
And death he seemed not fear
But to be reincarnated was far worse a fate
Than to be rejoined with loved ones at the pearly gates
Finally he had nothing left to pen
And talked of his passing with a friend
Upon the desk he left his pen to rest
As for himself he thought it best
To be laid to rest 'neath a pair of old pine trees
And said that it would be the end of Bixby
After more than a century his work of art
Has touched my heart
And by and by I think of him

Tina Nash
Abington, MA

I have been writing poetry for almost twenty years. I was inspired to write this poem after reading Memories and Other Poems *by Bixby. I wrote my own book of poetry in 2013,* Poetry: The Forsaken Art Form, *which is available through Barnes and Noble. I also have my own poetry web page at https://www.facebook.com/tinanash.poetry.*

Thank You Isn't Enough

Living with no hope destroys body and mind
Slipping into personality changes that aren't refine
Searching over and over is an endless task
Jaded again with no hope to grasp

Gone were the dreams that flowed through my veins
A powdery dust is all that remains
God in His mercy heard my heartfelt cry
An American hero was His staunch reply

Possessive of virtue like knights of old
Marked and chiseled in fibers of gold
Willing to trade his life for another
Lightning flash decision like no other

The words of his brave deed took my breath away
Burned in my memory to be replayed
Restored was my faith and veins flowed with new hope
Thank you could never describe this inner kaleidoscope

I penned these words for generations to read
How a brave deed can restore life's seed
This American hero touch God's hand
Making the stars and stripes forever stand

Nona Reedinger
Tower City, PA

The inspiration for this poem was Colonel John W. Horn — to think that something that happened overseas could have a profound effect on someone at home. God works in mysterious ways. Prayers are sent daily to all who guard our freedom.

Loving Hearts

My everything knows
He loved her with
All his heart.
She loved him, God-proud.

Confirm or deny,
Whichever way
It will go—
You know they will cry.

I didn't say my
Poetry was good—
I said that
They were published.

I found a dozen
Morels, graced
My orchard lot;
I ate them all up.

Constance Warren
Detroit, MI

I'm an eighty-two-year-old childless widow and live in Detroit, Michigan. I was an LPN for thirty years and before that served with the USMC. My mom read to us (poetry and other things) and I never forgot that. Looking around I see "fodder" for poems all around me. I love to read other poets' work as well.

Just a Person

I am not a champion, nor am I famous. I am
just a person. I am just me. I am loved by so many.
I am a writer of people, and their memories.
I am a writer of faith and good will for everyone.

I am not a champion, nor am I famous. I am a
writer who writes about things I love, and what I
or who I have lost on the way. I can see hope in
what I write. I am a writer of me. Writing my dreams,

And what inspires me to remember. I am not a
champion, nor am I famous. I am just a person who is
a writer. Someone that feels so much from everything
and everyone. Cries about what I believe in. Cries about

all the children that have fallen for no
reason. Their time always too short. I am a writer
with feelings to share, and to hide away. I believe in so
much around the world. I am someone who cares for all,

the living and the dead. I am not a champion, nor
am I famous. I am a writer who is a person who cares.
I am a writer for me.

Dianne Hill
Morris, IL

*The pleasure I get from writing is what makes me who I am as a person. I see
myself doing amazing things as a writer. My son and my husband believe in me
and that's amazing. With God and my son and husband on my side, there is
nothing I can't do.*

Spring

Weddings planned. Love abounds.
Birds build nests.
Bees buzz around.
Trees and flowers bud and bloom.
All creations come alive
When spring arrives
From winter's rest.

Storms, sunshine, humidity.
All a possibility.
As we begin our outdoor activity
Darkness gives away
To longer daylight
All because spring has arrived.

Gladys R. Witt
Hamersville, OH

My Little Kitty Cat

My little kitty cat came here to stay
Her baby soft fur seemed softer each day
She'd always meet me at the door then jump in my lap
Just petting her gently was where it was at
On cold winter nights she'd sleep on my bed
If really chilly, she'd curl up next to my head
For twelve wonderful years she shared our time
That was alright with me, her warm company was fine
But early this spring, our Lord called away
She's now mousing in heaven and happier I'd say
I miss her quiet purr and the feel of her fur
I loved my curly tailed KC, my little girl

Charles Patrick Foley Sr.
Rockford, MI

As I've gotten older my furry four-legged friends have become a close part of our family. This spring the best little cat passed out of my life. This poem was written in memory of that fuzzy little bundle of fun.

Silent Cries from the Heart

Can you hear me Lord?
My heart is heavy
The War has left scars deep within my soul
I feel abandoned and alone
Please hear my plea
I did my duty, I served my country
I need you Lord more than ever to walk with me
through troubled waters and unknown places
I have seen much, and can never forget my fallen comrades
May your heavenly light shine on the living giving hope
to all those in need
I place my trust in you, and pray for strength

Ellen A. Gaskey-Berryman
Virginia Beach, VA

I dedicated this Memorial Day 2015 to the members of the armed forces both living and deceased and in honor of my brother, Rick Heckmann.

Love

There is a force so strong,
So overwhelming,
So complex,
That it changes a person's life and thoughts.
With that force comes pain,
And crying,
And heartaches,
And memories of good and bad times.
There is no other force
That brings a person to the pinnacle of success
Or the lowest depth of failure
More than this force does.
Since the beginning of time
People have fought,
Lied,
Cheated,
And even died
For this force,
And still no one can yet define it.
For the force I am talking about,
Is the greatest force of all.
And that force is…
Love.

Stephen David Hart
Ojai, CA

I wish to dedicate this poem to my sister Diane Mary Hart.

The Illusion of a Portal

While sitting and thinking by a stream
My conscious being seemed to float in a dream.
I saw the image of a pine tree
On the water reflecting itself back to me.

It seemed I saw a spider's web
Woven 'round and 'round, then up and down,
Next back and forth to make a bed,
For a bug that appeared to be dead.

A leaf was hanging in the spider's trap,
Struggling to relieve itself of the web's grasp.
A bird's nest was above it in a bough
The birds were singing excitedly, flying free.

The pine needles hanging there were fluffy and green,
Moving like egret feathers floating on a stream.
The illusion of a portal, the spider's web, curled,
Pointing, beckoning me to a parallel world.

All of a sudden, I realized it could not be.
It was an illusion of my eyes, I see,
Reflecting the feelings hidden deep in me
That wanted to escaped this world and be free.

Oh, what a wonder, what joy I would feel,
If this current world would just let me flee,
Allowing me to enter that peaceful realm,
Where the spider's web was beckoning me.

Denise E. Bowlin
Shreveport, LA

Ten-Cent Philosophy

Sometimes we are sorrowful
Sometimes we, in joy, overfull
Sometimes ennui creeps up in a way so powerful
Sometimes sheer peacefulness becomes delightful

Sometimes, sometimes, sometimes —

And then, do we learn to cope
Do we use our brains in full scope
Do we self-acknowledge for ourselves to be no dope
So we untangle ourselves so we can feel some hope

It's a victory when we figure it out
Whatever it is, we know we're not just about
Goodness, mercy, and loving acts, all dispel doubt

And, so our lives move in one way or another, Ms. or Mrs.
My hope is only for the better way with no misses
Nothing else really matters, love not hate becomes the
  badness resister
Because, after all, we are finally everyone's forever sister

Helen-Anne Keith
Chelsea, MA

The Little Baby Brother

The first thing noticed are the eyes;
Darkly set they are a surprise.
The brow is rounded yet you know,
Later the family face will show.

Flags flying in joyful celebration.
Now's the time to inform the nation
Of a new baby brother; her new role today,
Holding and helping in every way.

Big sister going through simply can't resist
Touching his cheek with a flick of the wrist.
She has to keep busy, dusting, lots still to do,
And now she has to help mind baby, too!

So this is the new brother of which much is known,
He does a lot of sleeping, tucked up on his own,
Loved by all who pass him around.
He just sleeps on safe and sound.

Ann Gallant
Marshall, TX

*Such a gift to our family, these children have been giving me great joy. I try
to help a busy mother in any way I can. Technology now allows us to all stay
in touch, and photos fly around the globe. Big sister, Suvannah, and little
brother, Connor, will, I hope, be as close as my sister and I are.*

Ode to the Mountains

Broad rugged shoulders and snow covered tops,
    Your feet in green meadows 'neath golden sun;
Conspiring with him how the rest of us
    Should view this world and remember the past;
To gaze upon men whose dreams were mere
    Fancy, ready, set and willing to climb;
Your highest peaks or sailing seas that time
    And ambition bridge to shores of success.

In your strength and patience my days are filled
    Staring at your peaks and wondering if
Someone before me, centuries ago,
    Was as awestruck as me by your grandness?
In silence and majesty I am stilled;
    Your melting glaciers carry a message
Of gladness and hope for both strong and weak;
    Just looking up, I take another step,
Ever to seek and pursue life's journey.

Jeffery Moser
Aurora, CO

Unseen Variables

We fill spaces in time
on an ordinary planet
which revolves around
an ordinary star in an
ordinary galaxy among
billions of galaxies
with their stars and planets

But it is what
we do not see that
is just as true
as our macrocosmos
which contain some
of what we know

Truth also consists
of feelings such as hate
and love and dreams
and these truths will
continue as long as
there are in the microcosmos
sentient, intelligent, and
spiritual beings living in
life-giving systems

Allan Mohl
Ossining, NY

Hidden Sorrows

I am both seen and unseen.
Each day I smile yet most I want
to curl up and cry.

Unknown this pain of mine goes
to those in my life. Fear of being
a burden forever on my mind.

Smile when I wish to cry
laugh when I wish to hide
away.
Joke and push away, when what
I need is to be held and given a
few loving words.

This question a plague on my
mind. Why must it be this way?

Rachael Sill
Sandstone, MN

Amazing Things That Happen

Sunshine and roses,
What a beautiful scene it poses
A wonderful smile, makes your day worthwhile
The deer are playing in the field,
To watch them gives you such a thrill
I saw the blooming of a daffodil
When I was sitting on the hill
May joy and peace be to all
I heard the birds making their joyful call
Follow in God's light,
Then everything will be alright

Margie R. Chisom
Roanoke, VA

To Ella Faith

Oh Grandchild of mine I've waited so long
For you to be born so I can sing you a song
The stories I'll tell you will be of the past
Of people and memories that are meant to last
And now with the blessing of God's loving grace
I will be able to gaze upon your beautiful face
So Grandchild of mine be it ever so clear
I will love you forever and I'm so glad you are here.

Gail M. Wolf
River Grove, IL

Summertime

It gets so hot in the summer
you surely don't want to be
a plumber because of all of
the smell.
It will just make you not well.
You just want to relax
and do nothing. But
some of us have to work
so we don't become a
jerk.
Summer is when all
the animals come out
creepy crawlers and ones
with a snout.
Got to be careful not to shout
wake up people they will
be unhappy.
And then I will feel
crappy.

Betty Parry
Pawhuska, OK

I really enjoy writing poems. My great-grandfather started the trend. My dad was a great poem writer, as well. It warms my heart to know I can write poetry. It's a wonderful thing. I like making people happy. I love writing poems as a hobby. Writing poems is my favorite hobby.

Satisfaction and Joy

For some satisfaction is a good meal,
For others it takes a long trip abroad.
You are somewhat peculiar and weird,
If you merely want to watch a sunset.

There is life and lasting beauty for all to see,
But most people pass their life in darkness.
Many never try stopping to smell the flowers,
Perhaps foolishly cautious of phantom bees.

Yes, we shall always work and suffer,
Many even for a meager living wage.
But the best things in life are still free.
Joy visits the pauper as much as the rich.

Satisfaction precedes happiness,
Just like rain promises a rainbow.
Seek satisfaction on small things,
To enjoy a full life of lasting joy.

Whenever discouraged or angry,
Follow the advice of the artful ant,
Any obstacle to its forward journey,
Is promptly skipped to an alternate path.

Look carefully upon your daily life demands,
Any worthwhile task must provide satisfaction.
Seek the tiny spark of joy in every moment,
And satisfaction will morph into happiness.

Mariano A. Rivera
Maitland, FL

The Return

Divisions are dissolving
Coherence has begun
Our true essence is emerging
Conscious unity as one

Our soul no longer separated
Eternal happiness we embrace
The kingdom of Heaven now within
Spiritual enfoldment takes place

Into the great awakening
Through the outpouring light
Unfolds our new beginnings
To a place shiny bright

Blessed angels guide us
To our destination point
A mirror we represent
Of God's creation, anoint

Graduates we are
Carrying sacred codes within
Trusted with our commitment
Free from lies and sin

Part of a higher evolution
We forever strive to be
Searching for inner fulfillment
To find life's destiny

Sandra A. Young
Seneca Rocks, WV

A Shadow

As the green grass grows over me,
head to toe, where I lie,
what will you think as you walk by?
Close above me you will pass,
I will call out, but alas,
you hurry on by, then fade from view,
till all I see is a shadow of you.

Teresa Foster
Lott, TX

Saying Good-Bye

Today I found out that you were gone.
It left me wondering how we were going to say so long.
All the memories that we've had to share.
And all of the ways you showed us you cared.
We were just talking about our days when we were
Young and all of the adventures and all the fun.
Of horse back riding and sleep overs to.
We seemed to always have something to do.
Walking down that ole dirt road that took on
Adventures that were never told.
Oh how I'm going to miss you and will never forget
We love you, and miss you, but there's no regrets.

Frances Reid Morrell
Santa Fe, TX

Birthdays

Birthdays, the pages of time,
Look at your life —
See the sprinkling of frosty gray in your hair
The lines that appear on your face —
Your map of life lived.

Look into your eyes — see the secrets,
Told and forever untold.

See the young, foolish things
Good times, sad times
Time to face life —
To welcome new life, cry for the loss of life.

A birthday —
A time to remember times past —
To look to the future —
Remember, your birthday —
Another page in your life.

Go forward, do your best.

Josephine Ingalls
New Smyrna, FL

Tips Regarding How to Live Longer and Prosper

Living long and being healthy, too,
is critical to many, including me and you!
To achieve this end, however, much must be done,
including drawing closer to our own healthy chums!

Truly, who we hang out with may trump everything else,
so we need to reach out, and not just sit on a shelf.
Eating smarter is thought to be very important, too,
if we wish to be more robust as a general rule.

Next, seeking to define our own purpose in life,
is vital if we're going to overcome many sources of strife.
In addition, we need to exercise as much as we can,
if extending our lives is really our own personal plan.

These four notions are things that we all can do,
to live long and prosper for an extra decade or two.
But as we all know talk is really cheap,
unless we take action, and put in gear our dancing feet!

Thomas S. Parish
Topeka, KS

All points noted here were derived from Ginny Graves' "Cheaters Guide to Living to 100," published in Parade *on April 5, 2015. Notably, the secret to having a "good life" lies in what we do with it! More specifically, some say that we should "eat, drink and be merry, for tomorrow we die." However, for those who do wish to live longer and prosper, the points described in this poem may help them to better understand what they need to do, and with whom they need to do it, if they truly wish to be healthier and happier, and possibly live for an extra decade or two. Of course, whatever it is that you decide to do, it'll always be up to you!*

To a Special Person

To a very special person
Who I met over the years
I get to know you more each time we are together
You are one of a kind

You are a caring person
One who I am glad to know
You make me cheerful when I am down
You are a good friend to talk to

You can make daily cares melt away
Talking with you is a pleasant thing to do
You make me feel that I am special
Thank you for being you

The world is a hard place to be sometimes
With your support and kindness it isn't so bad
May you be happy and have lots of love in your life
I am glad to have you near

Donna Kimmel
York, PA

This Woman's Passion of Love

I breathed you in
Quenched my skin with your laden honey
Satiates a fire
Dripping more than desire

Coursing through these veins
Intertwining with my blood
Pumping no vital potions
Just cresting you and your love

Shores of impassions force
And sincerely returns
Only to the true source
In which it begun

Desperate as a school girl's crush
Crashing against her heart's shore
Crazed with passion and desire
Crying to be unrestrained
To you, the one she loves

The whimsies of a flicking child
An immature girl's intimate embrace
Graces through this woman's passion
For only you
To have and embrace

Shawndra Lyn Daniels
San Augustine, TX

My Father's Love for Me!

This is the story about a father's
heavenly love.
It all began, when God sent His
only Son from above.
Long before I was born, He knew
all about me.
I am so thankful to God for sending
Jesus, to set me free.
As He walked upon this earth, going
from place to place, He healed the
sick by His favor and grace.
Jesus loved me so much that He
found me, when I was lost.
He showed even more of His love,
when He paid the ultimate cost.
My Jesus loved me most, when
He laid down His life for me, on
the cross.
Jesus came to save and He did so,
by His blood that was shed.
All my sins were removed once
and for all on the third day,
when my Jesus arose from
the dead!

Heather R. Begley
Hernando, MS

*From the first time I ever heard Pastor Joseph Prince preach the gospel of grace,
I felt in my heart that it was the true gospel. The way he delivered the gospel of
grace and the unmerited favor of God only made me fall in love with Jesus so
much more. Now that I know I'm the righteousness of God in Christ, I'm blessed
in knowing that through Him, I'm destined to reign in life.*

Poetry

The poet in my soul
I didn't find until growing old
Then I looked at life with a different view
Then my life was made anew
Poetry spoke to my heart
Even the wind blowing had a part
The flowers brought more joy each day
As I walked along the poetry pathway
It's through the poems the flowers I see
Even the hum of the bee
The birds had a different design
When I saw them with my poetry mind
So poetry may you live on and on
Consider how you have grown
Poetry gives more than you put in
You can see where all you have been
You can see the future with a poet's eye
You can be a poet if you really try
Poetry comes from the heart within
All you have to do is begin

Kathryn Gardner
Greenbrier, AR

The Summer Storm

Thunder bowled across the heavens
The earth seemed to tremble in its wake
The sun suddenly disappeared from view
And granite gray clouds an appearance did make.
A gusty breeze began its journey
Traveling to who knows where
Swirling eddies of miniature dust clouds
Quickly began dancing here and there.
The rain came down in bucketfuls
Washing the land around
I wondered about the animals
Hoping not one would be drowned.
Then as quickly as it appeared
The storm clouds did scurry and go
The sun broke forth making rain drops glisten
Giving the earth a refreshing glow.
Seemingly the land had been christened
The flowers and trees did sparkle and shine
Air was fresh and very pure
The land again seemed safe and fine.

Virginia Fuhr
Oviedo, FL

Good-Bye

To Sophie Stepsay

Sunrise bloomed rose
In azure sky,
Like the day
My sister, Ilise, died.
I meant to wish her
Good luck with her
Neck operation,
But she died before I could.
Now I end all our good-byes
With, "I love you,"
Spoken as if it were our last,
For I want that
Sense of closure.
We are not promised tomorrow,
A sunrise blooming rose
In azure sky.

Richard Stepsay
Aurora, CO

Poverty's Litany

Asleep on the grass, wrapped in the dust of the city,
upside down sandals the pillow beneath his head.
His search for warmth and shelter now once more behind him.
The worn wooden park bench the roof of the vagabond's bed.
Tomorrow he'll breakfast on food overlooked by the trash man.
Tomorrow he'll look for cans he can turn into cash.
Tomorrow eye contact will probably once more elude him,
as he tries to convince those around him,
he is not human trash.
The seat of the bench, the roof of the homeless one's bedroom.
A plant the sprinkler has watered stands watch to the side,
poverty's exit grows smaller with each passing season;
acknowledged.
Acknowledging that, his hopes have withered
and died.

Shirley R. Turner
Escondido, CA

As a retired emergency room nurse, I find nothing so interesting as people. The ideas, behavior and interests of others is food for my study daily. I have been a military wife, mother, foster mother, and university instructor and still I love people more than any other interest or subject. Poetry, I feel, allows us to paint pictures of life and show ideas for consideration in very vivid colors. I am sure poetry is the distillation of life.

Will You?

Will you remember me when I am far away?
Will you look at my picture each night?
Will you send me letters
to let me know one day it will be better?
Will you listen to my hopes and my fears
if I have PTSD in the coming years?
Will you understand the reason
I have come to this far off place?
To fight for country and freedom —
Will I become a nameless face?
Will I be remembered just once a year?
This, above all, is my greatest fear.
Will you help me as I try to adjust
back to a life, I may no longer trust?
And if by fate, I don't come back to you,
will you still believe in what I tried to do?
Will you?

Shari K. Martinez
Lackwanna, NY

This is for all those who fought. Some were remembered — some were forgotten. I miss you.

Sink or Swim

Just treading water, barely afloat.
Not moving forward, in a lead coat.
Breathing's a challenge—where is the air?
Where are the people who should all care?
Pressure and squeezing, my lungs can't expand.
I'm sinking too quickly: "Requesting dry land!"

I relax each muscle; I just close my eyes.
Letting it all go, with one final sigh.
Expecting a flooding to wash over me,
I calmly accept what is to be.
A bright light surrounds, I think, "This is it."
When again I am upright, my body submits.
But, I take a deep breath, I open my eyes,
And I'm on the same beach, by the seaside.
The pressure subsided, my heart rate is calm—

I shook it off this time…

"Breathe in, breathe out."
Repeat the mantra to eliminate self-doubt.

Katherine O. Flower
Somerset, NJ

Reflections

To feel sadness is the linger of divinity.
To know the hurt of each page of your life is to
know the heart's certainty. But to accept
love makes you truly free.
If you cling to habit you will live in
predictability. Given to reside in hope
or folly. I linger soft shaded, but for
now let me feel the sun quietly in the
lullaby of air's and change the genesis
of my prayers.

Derek Walsh
Millis, MA

Peace: Our Window to Heaven

Peace is our window to Heaven
Ours to build though it takes a thousand years:
Replacing the rule of the tank, we use tools
To let new light shine, drying old rueful tears.

Peace is *our* window to Heaven
Though long the darkness has reigned,
New hands of new hope will build our new
Aperture: life's light: all feral by new light tamed.

L. J. London
Shaker Heights, OH

Sandy Hook School Tragedy

I could hear the children playing,
Their voices loud and clear.
Was time to start the school day,
With learning duties drawing near.
I could hear the children singing,
Majestic were the sounds I heard.
Beginning in the early morn,
A melody each one had shared.
I could hear the teachers softly praying,
Please don't harm these little ones.
Let us live to see tomorrow,
We can't believe our work is done.
I can see the throne in Heaven,
Twenty and six just entered in.
I can hear their welcome entrance,
Come in my child, eternal peace begins.
I can see the global cries of pain.
I can hear their loved ones pray.
We will see your face, hear your voice, feel your love,
All in painful memories to never fade away.

Joyce H. Pait
Southern Pines, NC

Treasured Memories

Memories come to mind
Like a special moment in time.

Memories coming to light again.
Memories left in the shadow where
Our love has been.

Memories, treasures of my heart
Kept dearly, closely.
Memories, lingering, since we have
Been apart.

Jewelean Taylor
McKenzie, TN

I challenged myself to write my poem, "Treasured Memories." I wanted to write it in a serious and romantic voice, one that we all can relate to because we have had similar memories. Perhaps we secretly wished for a second chance. Nonetheless memories of love left in the past will always be a time to remember.

Men

Men, you are our constant lovers,
making us women volatile rovers.
You just knowingly strut your stuffs,
it's alright, 'cause we still love your bluffs!
By showing off your wares,
you know what you have, who really cares!
Making us believe it's okay?
As we will honor your stay.
So don't go flaunting your derriere,
you may have a cliché in your résumé!
You men have such poor judgement,
but, we still love you through your amusement.
On just how we women think,
you are the "apple of our eyes," in a blink
so, do what you have been doing well,
the sexier you get rings a bell.
Let us be your ever-loving mentors,
with or without your sex detectors.

Gordon L. Wilcox
Kapolei, HI

Because

I want to know you.
I want to see you.
I want to put you in my heart!
As you put Moses in the cleft of a rock.
What cleft have you made for me?
Because of Jesus
I can look in your face
As you reveal yourself
Through your inspired word.
Your glorious light
Will always be
More than I can take in.
Please—what you put in
My head about you—
May I allow you to put
In my heart!

Myrt Offutt
Hot Springs, AR

Why Does It Rain on Sunday?

It started out like any day—
My news script in my hand.
My eyes perusing daily news
Involving this great land.
A little voice possessed my brain
I knew it sought a fun day.
To my surprise a question came,
"Why does it rain on Sunday?"
Nonplused, confused and at ill at ease
I pondered this strange quest
Of nature's trend to choose that day
In deference to the rest.

Then in a flash it came to me.
I found and knew the key.
The beauty of this nature act
Came clear as clear to me.
Ma Nature wants to cleanse the earth
As days and weeks go by
From Monday to the weekend run
Dirt grows and cakes and dries
The earth so badly needs a bath
That nature chose this one day
To cleanse it well with gentle rain
What better day than Sunday?

Lloyd S. Foote
Tempe, AZ

Circle of the Shaman

I have to compete always with reality,
and transcend accepted rational bounds.
So I have learned to purify with water,
and to drive out evil spirits with sounds.

Mythic voices cry to me from the thunder.
I can see visions in the sun with eyes opened wide.
Spirits visit me and bring answers from down under,
their supple shapes flowing over me like a tide.

The tribe sleeps below me as I search for the lost sun,
my mind distorted with flickering visions of doom.
This profession holds me hostage as with a gun,
confining me within a small circle within a smaller room.

As a child it was a warrior and warrior only I wished to be,
but my father was a shaman and his and his and now me.
So I bless the warriors and send them on their way.
They to do battle while with the women and children I stay.

When my people have no present need for my powers,
I sit in spiritual seclusion and count the hours.
They bring me food and drink and sit it before my door,
feeding me like a dog, then calling me forth like a whore.

I have to exist within myself in total isolation,
socially cut off from all members of my nation.
I watch them dance and listen as to one another they call,
while I sit here in my closed circle and hate them all.

Malcolm Lane
Camden, AR

God Made His World Technicolor

There are birds, all sizes, shapes,
Colors, and forms, but they are
Birds. So are dogs, cats, all
Other animals, and us human beings.

There are the beautiful colors of
The rainbow, the trees, flowers,
The sky, the stars, and the moon
That shines at night.

All things on Earth, as in Heaven,
Was created by him, and for him.
There is no doubt about it.
There is no other, like God's
Technicolor.

Beatrice Scurry
Cincinnati, OH

My inspiration is to help someone along the way to see and focus on God's beautiful creation, to encourage and reach out in love, and let them know that we are not on this life journey alone. I give God all the glory and all the praise. I love writing and putting my thoughts on paper.

Reflections of a Life

And in the shadow of the night, when evening comes and the loss
of light
My thoughts go backwards through the years to happy times and
childhood tears
Of broken dreams, and dreams come true
Of loved ones lost and found anew
Of hope and fear and joy and love and absolute faith in God above
I have no thought of things not done or what should be or races run
Only thoughts of peace and hope
Of reaching out my hand to help
Of reaching out my heart with joy
To brush away some hurt or tear
And leave some hope, where there was fear
This is all that can be done,
Not what we do before we die
All that's important is that we try
Amen

Ruth Schowalter
Santee, CA

*I have always liked poetry and writing. I didn't have much time when I was young.
I was the second oldest of ten children born during the Depression. I had to help
my mother raise my brothers and sisters. After I married, I gave all my attention
to my two sons. They have excelled in every way. My grandchildren have followed
in their footsteps. In my retirement, I started to write again. I wrote about thirty-
six poems about my early life. I called it "House of Memories." On November 14,
2015, I will be eighty-eight years old.*

Who Is She?

Please sir do not ask me who she is,
I do not have the words to say.
Often she travels abroad,
but with me she will always stay.

Yes we are friends,
her most guarded secrets with me she does share.
Yet we are more than friends,
I need her more than my lungs need the air.

Are we lovers then?
Does she drink from my lips in moonlight's embrace?
Our love reaches far beyond the flesh,
without her this cold world I could not face.

She is nothing to me,
who could ever own the sun?
But she is everything to me,
our souls are knitted as one.

Please sir do not ask me who she is,
our relationship goes by no name.
Though it cannot be spoken it will endure,
as long as Heaven and Earth remain.

Larry Hill Jr.
Shiloh, OH

I Want One

It's beautiful
I'll take it
In fact, I'll have two or three

Don't you
Just think
It will look great on me

I must have it
I will pay
Whatever fee!

Seriously?
You say
That is it free

I'll have to wear it
Everywhere
Because I want the world to see

Just how
Transforming
A smile can be

Leeann Kathleen Corrao
Hopewell Jct., NY

Bullet

I am a school
I hear the bullet go by,
I am a child
I hear the bullet go by,
I am a mall
I hear the bullet go by,
I am a movie
I hear the bullet go by,
I am a soldier
I hear the bullet go by,
The world has gone crazy
No flowers will grow
The world is black
I felt the bullet

Patricia Davidshofer
Columbus, NE

All Places Are Not Alike to Me!

Sometimes I creep. Sometimes I dance over the rocks.
I leap for joy over boulders.
I dance over rocks as I go through the canyons.
I leap for joy, tossing rafters through rapids.

I am an artery, a bloodline for creation. I nourish the flora and fauna.
I seep through the deserts. I quietly, smoothly flow through
the prairies…
nourishing, cultivating the grasslands filled with hayfields,
alfalfa, cattle, horses.

All places are not alike to me!
I am the river.

I undercut the banks. I chisel out canyons. I gouge gorges.
I knock over trees and carry them downriver.
I pile them like pick-up-sticks.
I carry soil and deposit it in unlikely places
where trees and flowers take hold.

I am God's engineer.
All places are not alike to me!
I am the river.

Jo Nelle Graber
Albuquerque, NM

Summertime

The snow was softly falling
The trees are in bloom.
Summertime coming soon.
Those cold raw days are coming
To an end.
Soon to be forgotten.
Green grass is growing.
We'll be playing. It's summertime.
Been a warm winter, but now it's bragging.
Those cold raw days are nagging.
The sun is high. The snow is melting.
Oh, it's going to be summertime coming soon.
The water is running
The children are splashing.
Their hands are clapping.
Summertime coming soon!
Those cold raw days are pushing
Me back again.
I can't wait! Summertime.
My mind turns to the gardens
Lawns to mow.
Weekends at the lake.
Busy all the time
When it's summertime.
Oh, it's going to be summertime
Coming soon.

Melvin Peter Wenstad
Michigan, ND

It was the earliest of springs, here in North Dakota, and even some planting had taken place in March. Then came some cold raw days. It looked like it was going to be our normal April, but warm spring days persisted to be one of our most delightful springs that I can remember. I'm sixty-eight this year! I grew up on a poor farm in the Turtle Mountains of North Dakota. I have labored and labored to be a carpenter—a big subject for me, and I'm happily still at it and still learning.

Tarnished Halo

Polishing my tarnished halo
trying to make it shine,
changing the skeleton past,
amends made,
in first sight,
my halo is tarnished,
been for years,
I looked in the mirror
cried a thousand tears
fell to my knees,
aura all tattered,
my soul is torn,
I have to change this life,
so innocent at first born,
no beauty I see,
caught up in the fast lane,
speeding at 103
love yourself first
then your family
wins your soul a Grammy
have life's map to follow
it's like I've been awakened
from a bad dream,
my aura a kaleidoscope of colors
Halo is sparkling gold,
my life safe and not stolen

Cathy Tibbetts
Pomeroy, OH

Indescribable

At what point do I express
What you truly do for me
It's indescribable how you make me
Into the person I want to be

You're my tour guide of His lessons
Carrying me along
Knowing you will never drop me
Even when I'm wrong

Your heart's passion to help others
Captivates me the most
It's what ties us together, fits like a glove
And makes us so close

I search for a secure world
Yet still long to venture
Your arms are my safe haven
And your heart is my adventure

Your love for me is so pure
But your love for God is greater
This love can even change the world
All thanks to our creator

Melissa Gecewich
Parma, OH

This poem was inspired by my husband. While we are still within our first year of marriage and considered "newlyweds," this man has encouraged, motivated and captivated me more than anyone ever has in my life. I am blessed beyond words to begin this journey with Adam and I am thankful for the support he has given me in every aspect of my life.

Pain

Tears
Feel like spears
To my very core

What we could have had
Travel
Plans unravel

Blank stares
Looking at me
Not knowing

I am the love of his life
Friend and wife

Pain
Strain
Must we bear it?
God be with us
Touch
Hold
Secure our future

Death will come
In its own time

Peggy S. Collier
Canyon, TX

Encore

You've been gone for a long while now you're
back with an enchanting smile

How I've missed your warm caresses upon my face
your gentle fingers running through my hair

The warmth of your soft embrace comfort me
while I enjoy the beauty that surrounds me

I gaze into the blue sky above and soon I
realize once again you'll be gone

But I'll always wait for your return, for each
year at the same time and place you'll come
back with such unforgettable sweet and soothing
pleasures

This special love of mine which I speak it's
spring at its peak

Barbara A. Kelley
Detroit, MI

I love life and its given rewards that come my way each morning when I awake from my nightly slumber. I give thanks to my Lord and Savior, along with Dr. Rev. E. S. Payne, my senior pastor of 103 Young and my co-pastor, Rev. Charles E. Boles. I know nothing is promised, but through God all things are possible. I live my life obeying those righteous rules and I battle life's ups and downs along with the good and bad by embracing it with understanding, communication and prayers expressing my love for life and its blessings.

The Early Morning Rising

It smells so sweet and enterprising.
Dew is on the ground, the
Sun is shining down.
I behold all this!
With no reason to frown.
Soaking it up,
My head in the clouds,
Exhilaration, enthusiasm
On my face!
Life in its own way solved
My case.

Joseph Mercer
Garysburg, NC

"The Early Morning Rising" is the first poem I wrote. It came to me in a public building in Ahoskie, NC. I felt an inward peace come over me and I began to write. It seemingly came out of a clear blue sky. It was written around the early eighties as I felt inspired. Thank you for hearing my story. It takes me back to younger days.

Cry of the Children

There's a silent song of despair that whistles in our ears
It's the innocents yearning to be heard
A cry of those too young to comprehend,
Their frail lives weakened by the greed of man
A blackened sun shines down upon them
Their lives bleeding of hope and peace
Bodies enlarged by lack of sustenance,
Minds hungry for knowledge and understanding
No longer burns the fire inside their soul
Only the burning embers of despair remain
Hearts longing for the love of others
Fall asleep with the pangs of hopelessness
When will we hear the soft melody that rings in our ears
The cry of those longing to be heard
When does the heart soften to understand
That we are them and they are us
Never were we separate entities
Residing at different levels of existence
But rather one in union with creation
We are the light that dispels the shadows
Of silence in their broken world
Hope, peace and love are the gifts abiding within,
If only the gateway of desire were open
The hearts of the gods weep with a sigh
Wondering when will we hear the children's cries

Kim Davis
Jersey Shore, PA

Gifts

The day we were born we were given gifts
Gifts of life, time and love
Bestowed on us by the unseen hand
Who looks on down from up above
The gift of life is ours to use
To help ourselves and others
Not given to abuse
The yesterdays are behind us
What's happened there is done
When we awake tomorrow
A new day will have begun
Push aside your worries
Put them in days gone by
For now you're in tomorrow
And maybe now you'll find our why
The time that's been given is ticking away
The minutes, the hours,
Then gone another day
Daily and slowly the time disappears
The days, the months then go the years
So let's live our lives with malice towards none
Wake in the morning feel the warmth of the sun
Love your neighbor, your family
And the gates will open wide for you into eternity

Jim De Lisa
Wayne, NJ

My Heart Is Broken

My heart is broken
You left me too soon, don't you see
A piece you took to Heaven, a piece of
   my heart with the key
So humble, beautiful, caring,
So lucky to call you Mom

My heart is broken
As I listen for your song
You're in the wind, the trees
And a gentle, gentle breeze,
That caresses my cheek like a kiss,
Oh Mom, how do I do this?

I feel you in the rain
The sun on my face
The fragrance of flowers
I will be blessed by your grace

Family, friends and others
So lucky to know your "touch"
My heart is broken,
I miss you so much

My heart is broken
Too soon for me here below
For I lack the faith and peace
To which you came to know

My heart is broken
No longer your hand to hold
To guide me from my troubles
And keep me in your fold
My heart is broken

Rebecca Lohrbach
Mantorville, MN

My mother passed away on March 31, 2015. Struggling with the grief, shock and this life changing event, I sat down and started to write. I love and miss you forever, Mom!

Success of Me

I'm a success and through
my artistry, I've brought to
light the best of me.
Success can be measured
through my sight by each
day and night, I continue
on my journey for the best
things of this life.
Promises of old and goals
of the new this makes me
do what I do.

Berry Robinson
Pittsburgh, PA

I have the will to share my poetry. Please go to www.changes3.com and pick up my poetry book. My poetry is inspired by deep emotions from the soul that needed to be released.

Vietnam War

The people we thank,
The people who fought for us,
The people in the Vietnam war.
The people who died for us,
Gave their life for us,
We thank you for what you've done for us.
The men who saved us,
The ones who were scared,
The ones who were nervous.
The ones who didn't feel anything,
The people who had family that cried.
The people who had husbands and dads that died,
In the Vietnam War.
We love you all.

Amanda J. Olson
Wahpeton, ND

Seasons Parade

Springtime is here, crocus are in bloom
daffodils still underground, will be sprouting soon.
Tiny leaves upon the trees, weeks before were bare.
Some will soon bear blossoms, beauty beyond compare.
Animals are everywhere, jumping around with glee.
Birds singing sweetly, makes me happy as can be.
Summer is for fun and games and hearing nature's croon.
Sweethearts sit outside at night and gaze up at the moon.
Crickets make their melody and fireflies light the sky.
We hear loud claps of thunder and know the rain is nigh.
When we are at the ocean the waves slap at the shore.
The noise is so peaceful, it often makes us snore.
Autumn leaves are so beautiful, many different hues.
Red, yellow, brown and green and the sky is vivid blues.
I'm feasting on such bounty, veggies, fruit and such;
My orchard and garden was wonderful producing very much.
The animals as well as I are working very fast,
Stocking food for winter hoping it will last.
Winter snow falling softly, makes me want to sleep.
Then comes the howling wind making snow piles deep.
Tomorrow brings the sunshine making crystals on each tree.
Oh! The beauty that I behold can't be measured by degree.
May I always know the wonder of the beauty God has made,
And joyfully march forward in the seasons great parade.

Oma L. Graham
Princewick, WV

*I am a widow of three years. I spent twenty years as an Army wife and traveled
extensively. I have two sons, one daughter, six grandchildren and two great-
grandchildren. I am a retired LPN. I have three acres-plus of land and watch and
learn the habits of many animals and birds. I love the seasons which prompted this
poem. I can see God's work in everything. I love to sing, pray and give Him praises.*

Gone Fishin'

Up here, the water's clear and calm
No waves to rock my boat
There are fish galore
And nothing more
To do but throw a
Line and wait

Up here, the sky is
Always blue
No storms to wash me out
No need to stop, no need to sleep
Nothing to complain about

Up here, God saved this spot for me
No waiting when I arrived
Try not to miss me very much
I've never felt so alive
You'll see me soon, but
As for now
God's with me in this boat
And there's only room for two

Whitney B. Bevins
Gate City, VA

On May 9, 2015, my best friend lost his father to a tragic boating accident. A few days after the funeral, I was sitting at my desk trying to figure out what I could do to help him grieve. I got the sudden urge to get a pen and paper and the words flowed out of me of their own accord. There is no doubt in my mind that God Himself wrote this poem and He used me as a vessel. My hope is that this poem will mean as much to others as it does to me.

Unicorn

My desire to penetrate her mind
Matches my desire to penetrate her body.
The rarest of combinations,
She awakens within me the most
Primitive of urges.
With ease I could sink into the
Deepest parts of her,
Forgetting the dark cold life I've lived
Without her sunlight.
Her magic transcends the naked eye
Pushing my other senses almost to
The point of climax.
Sadly, she will never be mine.
Both a blessing and a curse,
Her beauty will always be in my
Presence but out of my reach.
She will forever remain the brightest
Light in my moonlit sky.

Hector D. Basora
Yonkers, NY

The Commute

We are the consummate commuters.
Committed Commuters,
Following orders,
Following dreams,
Following gods.
Enduring the traffic of life.
Till the end —
The traffic light of death.

Camille Einoder
Chicago, IL

Watching the endless trudging line of commuters tightly marching off the Metra trains, marching solemnly toward their destination somewhere down that long corridor to the street, made me realize slavery has not been abolished. We are living in that silent film, Metropolis.

Spring

Oh, if I could make those moments last
When hope no longer beyond grasp
Returns once more in early spring
To raise me high on angel's wing —

Oh, if I could make those moments last
When Cupid's arrows move too fast
While Earth inspired by her dream
Creates new life-forms deep within —

Oh, if I could make those moments last
And never let the season pass
How sweetly then this bard would sing
Of nature reborn yet again
Emerging like a floral queen
In love with every living being —

Lisa G. Manning
Gloucester, MA

Unlike the gradual arrival of spring which I experienced growing up in Stuttgart, Germany, here in New England, this season comes upon us almost unexpectedly after a usually very long, harsh winter. In my poem, I tried to express the renewed sense of hope and joy I feel during this time and my longing to hold onto this feeling forever. When I write my songs and poetry, I am seized by the same feeling, as though eternal spring reigns within me to "raise me high on angel wings." May my poem bring some hope to the reader as well.

Friends

Solo walks up a hill or down a long hallway,
seem endless and tedious at the end of the day.
How brief those same journeys become instantly,
with a like-minded friend walking right next to me.
We chat, laugh, and stroll and in no time at all,
we're back where we started—just how, don't recall.
How light heavy burdens become when they're shared,
with a friend 'cross the hall 'cause you know that they cared.

Millie Swigart
Canton, OH

I live in a retirement facility in Canton, OH. One day my neighbor suggested we walk together to collect our mail. Our facility is being updated, and retrieving our mail required us to walk a little further than normal to pick it up. My neighbor suggested I write a poem about our little jaunt, so I did. This one's for you, Polly.

This Life

All through the years of history
There has been fact, fiction and mystery
Only the characters have changed
Now our times seem so deranged
Look at how we have evolved
And yet nothing is resolved
What happened to peace and love
Now has turned to hate and crime
People homeless, starving and cut down in their prime
So much technology out there
Spend one on one together how dare
Nowadays a babysitter is a TV
My Lord no wonder this country has gone crazy
We live our days like the Indians and cowboys
Look these guns are real not toys
Some people looking for fake thrills
You find it from within not from
A needle or pills
What is happening to mankind
We have sight but appear to be blind
For if we all give from within
Our future generations can live and love again

Deborah Kathman
Cincinnati, OH

Camping Trip

Going camping we've been yearning
Driving to Hocking Hills we go churning
Pebbles flying rubber tires turning
Dodging potholes I'm finally learning
Climbing steep hills listening to oldies
Praying puppy evades nausea on this journey
At last pulling under the old evergreen pine tree
Wayne, Preshihs and me as clock chimes three
We pile out stretching our limbs
Neighbor Brown hollers, where y'all been?
Before long steaks sizzling on grill, coffee's in the pot
Gee whiz, this July weather is scorching hot!
Think maybe I'll take a dip in pool
No time we're antiquing put away the bar stools
Preshihs all cozy snoozing nary a sound
We head to town acting like two clowns
Upward downward terrain with many sharp curves
These mountain roads are testing my nerves
Reaching corporation sign — traffic heavy — I stop with a jerk
Getting my ice cold soda all over my skirt
Purchasing antiques packing safely in trunk
It's just what we needed — loads of more junk
Darkness approaches with a campfire all aglow
Roasting hot dogs on sticks and toasting yummy marshmallows
Twilight brings music of frogs and crickets in the night
Lying awake gazing high above at the sky — I love my life!

Patricia Ann Burchett Wilson
Marysville, OH

Writing is an enjoyable pastime for me. I've submitted two poems and I'm excited both have been published. A family genealogy book, Warpathawk Clan Legacy, *a tremendous endeavor, has been completed and distributed to twenty-five family members. The second book,* Coal Miner's Daughter, *details my childhood memories growing up in Southern WV coal mining country. Both books were dedicated to my parents, Claude and Martha Burchett, who instilled a message in me long ago: You get out of life what you put into it. I've strived to do well, whatever life offers.*

So This Is Sorrow

So this is sorrow; so this is grief.
Heart-weary, heavy-laden—Oh Lord! Where is relief?
How can we bear when wife and children weep
For sudden loss of husband, father,
Whom Jesus took to keep?

How do you bear the young wailing cries
Of those precious little ones who find Daddy has died?
What do we do when life must go on?
When we feel time should stop
Because our loved one is gone?

O praise to the king who holds every tear,
And whispers His love through friends and family dear.
So amidst this pain and grief and sorrow,
Let us find love, hope,
And joy for tomorrow.

Sarah E. Dake
Niota, TN

My Savior

I went my merry way today
Wishing Merry Christmas to all
Did I stop and think of Jesus
Being nailed to that cross
The price he paid for each of us
Only God could ever know
Then my heart was broken
As I stood there in the snow
For who could be any cleaner
Than the Lord who loved us so
The thorns that pierced his head
I cried when I thought of him
As I bowed down my head
Could I ever show my love for him
In a way to let him know
Yes I could put it on paper
So all the world could see
My love for my Savior
Who shed his blood for me

Gloria R. Smith
Lyons Falls, NY

It is with the utmost gratitude that I give thanks to our Father for the promise of John 3:16. Now smile, it's your road map home.

Scoutmaster

Humbly before this man I stand
When I was young, he took my hand

To guide me on life's rocky path
He taught me skills that I would need
To chart life's path to things unseen

May I honor his guiding light
And hope I pass his knowledge bright
To other scouts along life's path

For if I learned his lessons right
I only add to his guiding light

So those who follow may see
The path
To guide them on their journey
Through life

John R. Bentley
North Wilkesboro, NC

I have been in Scouts for sixty-seven years. I know the value of the scoutmaster in young men's lives. I have thirteen boys who earned their Eagle rank with my help. I will always be their scoutmaster.

You...

I see the stars, sparkle in your eyes
I hear the power in your voice when you open up your lips to speak,
My inspiration you are...
I sit in front of a blank canvas and your face these brushes begin
   to form
I sit staring down at a blank page, and my hands begin to scribble
   words about you
My inspiration you are...
I open my mouth to speak, but your presence intimidates me
I watch the way you interact with the rest of the pack and I
   contemplate on how I wish to press my lips against yours, but I
   am not that bold...
My inspiration you are...
My body longs for you to be in my bed
I listen as you speak and I swear I would not dare miss a beat, I go
   home to replay it all in my head
My inspiration you are...
Your smooth melanin skin, your pearly white teeth
Your perfect button nose
I really wish to hold you close
You will read this and fail to realize it is about you
My inspiration you are!
My inspiration is you!
The way you fight to the finish is why I love you
The way your word is your pride
My inspiration you are
The way your eyes shine when you reach your goals
The way you remain determined
The way you long for success
My inspiration you are...
My inspiration is you...

Wendy Mybell Napoleon
Brockton, MA

A Walk on the Beach

Have you ever walked along the beach
And seen the sandpipers run in front of your feet.
And heard the waves as they roll in.
And seen the sunset as night comes in.

Have you heard the seagulls as they fly about.
And felt the water as it splashed in and out.
The sand is so warm from the sun of the day
And so is the water as it splashed away.

The waves seem to talk if you listen you'll hear.
They're sending their message into your ear.
I have seen the sunset and the sandpipers too.
I have heard the waves and their voices of the blue.
The peace that you find as you're standing on the shore,
Is a peace that you will not find nowhere else
I am sure.

Neva Rootes
Largo, FL

Live for Each Day

Live each day like it's your last.
Tell your loved ones that you love
them, and show them your affection
with tender hearted words, hugs
and kisses, and especially your
actions.

Don't wait til tomorrow, for
tomorrow isn't promised and you
may miss the chance to see them
once again.

Don't let each day go by neglecting
the only chance that you may have
to make the best of yourself
and the opportunities you have.

So don't let each day pass like
the wind that blows by, instead
be thankful to God and live
each day like it's your last.

Rick B. Jimenez
Modesto, CA

My name is Rick B. Jimenez. I'm forty-eight years old and live in Modesto, California. I was inspired to write this poem after the passing of my grandmother. Her passing made me realize that I should value and live each day of my life to the fullest, showing those dear to me that I love them constantly. I also realized that I should look for and take advantage of every good opportunity that comes my way, so that I can be the best I can be and achieve my maximum potential and make a difference in other people's lives.

Something About Spring

When did it happen?
When did the self-hate, the negativity,
The pain, the non-existent confidence fade?
Because I woke up this morning,
And for the first time in a long time,
I saw beauty. I felt it had worth. I felt loved.
There must be something about spring.
About the new birth that comes along.
But there is something about time, too.
It's cliché really, "Time heals all wounds."
But when I see your smiling face,
And feel the love in your touch,
And I look in the mirror,
But don't hate what I see.
When I can see my past,
Not as a mistake, but as experience.
I see the good memories
Shining through the darkest times.
And I know.
The worst is over.
Problems will still come,
But being here, safe, loved…
I know that I survived.
I am beautiful, confident, important.
I always was, but now I can finally see it.
There must be something about spring.

Denisha Irene Burton
Falmouth, KY

Do Unto Others

We pledge our lives for better or worse,
We fall, we rise, we stumble, we curse.
Some loves last — most loves don't,
It can't be said which will or won't.

We rail in anger and vent our ire
With faces red and eyes of fire.
How dare you infringe upon my space!
I'll knock you down; I'll spit in your face!

Why can't we all just get along?
You don't get there simply by singing that song.
The television almost makes it a joke —
Share the love, buy the world a Coke.

The Sunday Christians will tell you this:
Profess like us and you can't miss.
Why does God endure all the religion
If there's only one way to get to Heaven?

I don't pretend to understand
What's happening in the hearts of man,
But I know one thing as everyone should.
There's tremendous power in doing good.

We each can find our different way
To do some good, and I'll just say:
Do that good and you will find
Love fills your heart and peace soothes your mind.

R. Hall Gilmore
Hartford, AL

Clouds of Concrete

Clouds of concrete,
    they roll and ponder past me
    they shield the sky of deceit
and hold a sunshine for all to see.

Clouds of concrete,
    nimbly pass the blue rotunda
    hiding at its other door a blackened nebula:
where there they turn to icy comets.

Clouds of concrete,
    they signal up to something more,
    so filled with promises, and torrential
    downpours
and onward they commune.

Clouds of concrete,
    they fall to earth with gentle sob,
    they hide our troubles with morning fog
and they cling together with hope and heat.

Clouds of concrete,
    cirrus winds and stratus fears
    they look down to us with held back tears,
condemned to forever wander the sky blue pavement,
concrete clouds of mind and patience.

Saul Yoshua Hirshbein
Weston, FL

Misfit Toys

In the land of misfit toys. Misfit! I am not a toy. Wow, I felt
like one of those toys in the land of misfit. The land, my
home, I was not wanted because there was something wrong
with me. Something weird. Look! He has a head
with eyes, a nose, a mouth, two arms, two legs. Does he
bounce? Let's see. No he doesn't. It just hit the floor and cries, can
he fly?
Let's see, throw it, no he just hit the floor and cries.
Can I punch it and will it come for more? Let's see, punch it, no
it just bleeds and cries more and more what is he good for? He's
no fun. I don't want it anymore. Leave him
on the floor.
Waited for the day to end
and for someone to come and bring me into a land
of wanted toys.
I, a young boy in this land of misfit toys waiting to put a end
to the unwanted one. The
weird toy that doesn't
fly or return to get
punched over and over or bounce up
and down just cry
and hit the floor.
Where is that Rudolph
with the red nose?
To bring me out of
the land of misfit…

Wilfredo Gomez
Brooklyn, NY

My name is Wilfredo Gomez. I wrote a book called Grenade at My Feet, *about
how I overcame life's worst challenges. I have three daughters: Yadira Gomez,
Liz Gomez, Clara Benitez. Miguel Pinero inspired me to keep on with poetry. He
was my cousin, a playwright, actor, and co-founder of the Nuyorican Poet Café.
He wrote the play,* Short Eyes, *and was nominated for New York Critics Circle
awards. He showed me that whatever obstacles get in the way, fight and overcome
every bad situation with writing poetry. I'm also inspired by my wife, Sendia
Gomez, author of "The Book Sight Within Me Through Poetry."*

Cry

I cry without shedding tears,
shy I am without letting it known.
Hiding myself and my needs so no
one would know.
Breaking into tears that only
my heart would know.
I do not lack love as I love
everyone.
I do not hate anyone only the
badness of some that should
let their heart know,
and ask themselves, why I cry,
and their hearts will let
them know.

Claro C. Feliciano
Culebra, PR

Candlelight

Good people are like candles
Burning themselves up to bring others light
As such, their lives are short ones — but they blaze ever so bright.
Their hearts warm us with their brilliant yellow light,
If only for a short time.
They shed their light over everything they touch
They teach us hope, they teach us love.
They burn brightest in the darkness
When all our faith has faded away; they bring us to the dawn,
Bathed in their gentle rays.
In daylight, when we need them not
We tend to douse their flame
Lighting them again, in darkness, fear, and rain.
Day in and day out we treat them in this way,
Yet still, they remain faithful,
Loving us the same.
When at the end
We've used them up,
Their wax is melted down,
Their wick marred in the muck,
Their light fades from this world.
Burning low, and disappearing quick,
They leave a much darker place
Stuck here in their wake.

Felicia Kelly
Corbin, KY

Home

An ode to KAP

One of the ways we measure wealth
Is by the size of our diamonds.
Not the rocks we inlay in gold,
But the infields we outline with chalk.
We know to polish and protect this—
The crown jewel
Of a rusting, old mill town
That we still stubbornly call
Home.
No wonder baseball is played on a diamond.
It is one of our greatest
Romances. We are married to it,
Engaged with the nuances of it.
It is a fairy tale for children:
Dreams of little boys
Who court the thought
Of joining the greats just by taking that trip
Home.
The magic of the game is the space between innings
When the other fans become your eccentric cousins,
Who all share your heart
In the form of that scuffed, leather ball.
And you realize that the place
Your team is sprinting for
Is where you have already arrived:
Home.

Rachael M. Wigton
Butler, PA

"Home" is dedicated to Patrick Reddick, Director of Communications and Interns, in the Butler BlueSox front office. I am forever grateful for his willingness to be my mentor, in writing and baseball, rather than just my boss. Thanks are also due to the other college interns, high school volunteers, and permanent staff members who I was privileged to call my colleagues. My short time with the BlueSox gave me friends and memories for a lifetime. I could never thank them enough for making me feel like part of the team and giving me the chance to call KAP "home" (butlerbluesox.net).

Who Knows?

Who was driving that fast-traveling train?
The one that made news for weeks on end.
Nobody knows. Inspectors keep assuring us doubters!
Observers still swear, "We know!"
But I'm still thinking, "Nobody really knows!"
I still want to definitely know: *the final end!*

Life spins and spins. I'm sure it will eventually stop.
Like the toy attached to a yo-yo string.
But when will the world stop spinning?
Answer me that, then I think I will know *everything.*

I want to know things such as:
Who's in charge of political stuff?
(The White House, for example…)
The one that sits vacant,
While the gang is at play? And
Who was flying that plane that "flew away?"
And stayed "away," even to this very day.
Where did those jailbirds hide?
After they broke out of prison?
That's really not what I want to know.
                    I want to know
When will our world stop its "go"?

LaVerne Foltz
Tucson, AZ

Foibles of Aging

I have just reached the age of ninety-five
But you know, it isn't easy staying alive.
I may tip over backward or fall on my face
And heaven forbid I should hasten my pace.
I'm proud of my hearing. I hear every word.
But those who repeat don't know that I've heard.
My memory is good and I'm really quite well
But strange things happen I can never foretell.
I may take off my glasses when they aren't even there
And brush my teeth when I should brush my hair.
I brew my coffee in a clear glass pot
But when it is colorless, it's the coffee I forgot.
Should my kitty be missing and can't be seen
I know I have locked her between the door and the screen.
Oh the foibles of aging. How will I survive?
But if I do, I may live to be one hundred and five.

Margaret Keyes
Mesa, AZ

Usually I don't take kindly to "old people" jokes. At my age, living in the modern world can be extremely frustrating and anything but funny. I realize we need to laugh at ourselves — and I do. All the events mentioned in "Foibles of Aging" have actually happened to me and I find humor in them in spite of myself.

Why?

You let your chances pass you by
For this careless choice you are going to cry
You had me there by your side
Begging you to please hold me tight
Instead your hurt and anger made you fight
Even though in your heart you knew it was not right

I felt your anger and disgust
And ran away in fright into the night
I felt your torment deep, deep inside
My heart felt your pain mount like the bursting of the tide

I always felt you had so much power over my life
That you would always help me decide my future strides
But your outbursts scared me, oh, so much, I had to run
Away and hide
My own sweet love, you are in a mood so dark, I feel
You cannot see the light
And you will never come back to hold me tight

If you could not control your emotions to be by my side
All the problems of everyday living would be too much to fight
To part, was the hardest thing to do, in my life
To never hold or have you by my side
Was a pain so deep, sometimes I could not hide
But it must be done, I really have to stay out of your sight
You will find someone who will make you feel alright
I'll do the same, but I will always wonder, why, when
You had your chance, why didn't you just hold me tight?

Stella B. Angulo
Peoria, AZ

Marshmallow

(perfect edition for the group to hear)

Marshmallow
cleans the
harsh yellow
on my teeth
It becomes
hard and mellow
sweetening every bite
blocking the dark night
of a missing tooth

Marshmallow
can be the
yellow hello
of the sun's new day
softening the blow
of too much heat

Marshmallow
can be the
car's cello
on the car radio
a soft seat
for the heartbeat

Walker Hayes
Columbia, MO

I've always been pro-choice, pro-accomplishment. I've never been anti-accomplishment. I loved 60s educator John Holt because he was pro-choice. I think the champion in sports should be the best team over the long-haul instead of the tournament winner! But pro-tournament never compromises on anything! I'm sick of being misunderstood! My poetry helps me communicate my feelings and opinions.

The Light in My Life

My insides crumbling little by little
Darkness taking over my life and body
Fading quicker and quicker, I can't fix what's wrong
No one can, here it comes again
The shaking, trembling
I can't breathe
I awake to being sick and gasping for air
Oh the pain, the pain is setting in
My head feels like it's been hit
My muscles ache
Is another coming?
And there you are
Your comforting touch, hands caressing me
Soft whisper in my ear telling me I'm okay
The only light I have through all the dark spells
The only thing to keep me going
My rock, holding me tight
Always trying to keep the bad away
But catching me when I'm falling in the darkness
And lighting up the way
Breathing air into my lungs, so I can see clearly
Thank you for being my light in this life
For trying to heal the darkness through this broken body
At times
It is because of you I can move on and be strong
No matter how long this darkness stays in my life

Jennifer Parisi
Agoura Hills, CA

"The Light in My Life" was written about my daddy and best friend. I don't know what I would do without you. I love you.

Suddenly Become

Unprepared but gladly ready,
Restrained yet strangely urgent,
Practiced but disengaged,
As parents of almost parents.

Drawn into an intimate distance,
Only measured in fleeting years.
Idle while a loved one labors,
In pains and push and tears.

Their pain yields to boundless joy,
Through tears it's crystal apparent,
Be it precious girl or boy,
You suddenly!
Suddenly, become a grandparent.

Bob North
Waynesboro, PA

Our family has expanded to include four children and, as of now, six grandchildren, hence the poem.

A Tribute of Volunteers

To give of one's free will and soul,
of heart, of mind and more untold.
To give of time, labor, gifts, affection,
advice, unconditional love, attention.
To ask for nothing in return
to teach, to reach and also learn
About the pain and hurt of others
with hopes of making brighter tomorrows.
It comes from love for one another
to live as keeper for our brother.
It's courage, care and love inspired
that carries volunteers through even when they're tired.
This tribute is to you who volunteer
who ask nothing in return but to bring cheer
To those who sometimes need a hand
a word, a smile, one who will stand.
To a volunteer it's one of life's greatest pleasures.
To the receiver a timeless, priceless treasure.
This can't be measured on any scale.
The strength within by no means frail.
We're thankful you give that part of you.
For volunteers are just a chosen few.
And on that very special day
the Maker will no doubt lovingly say,
"Enter in my good and faithful servant."
To all who volunteer they're words well meant.

Jesusa J. Perez
Brownwood, TX

*Having volunteered in various organizations, I understand the concept of a giving
heart. My inspiration for this poem came about through my job as a corrections
officer at a juvenile facility. As employees, there wasn't enough time to interact
with the youth. Volunteers made time to visit them. They listened to them with
nonjudgmental love, care and concern. The detainees responded well with improved
behavior and self-esteem. I wrote this poem honoring these volunteers and had the
privilege of reading it at a ceremony given in their honor. Thank God for all
volunteers. They're a reflection of His unconditional love.*

Longings

There's a missing link in my life's chain
An empty feeling that came to remain
A nebulous tedium lately came
I need to define it—give it a name.

Are people missing? A novel event?
I feel the loss of days that were spent.
They're gone from my life, past, I repent
What remains are unknowns, that's my lament.

Being molded by history a new mixture I weave
Continuing writing, quiet I achieve.
I persist in learning, no longer to grieve
Days that are gone, I still can achieve.

Continuing growth I make decisions
Not much is firm, I make some revisions
Creating my path without collision
Accomplish new goals I envision.

Denise Hengeli
Plantation, FL

The Pool

Meet me underwater
where smiles turn buoyantly
upward and bubbles leak
out one by one.
Our eyes lock, a joyful
gaze exchanged — for only
we know the secret,
silent, reverence of an
underwater rendezvous.
Fervently our legs kick,
propelling our bodies to
the surface, giddily gasping
for air; but we allow only
one second before submerging
again and again.

Susan Williams
Orlando, FL

Susan Williams is a freelance writer currently residing in Orlando, FL. She received her degree in English from Rollins College. Her life is filled to the brim with male energy right down to the dog. Susan's husband and two sons just make her better.

Winds of War

Like the phoenix into the heavens,
Youth arises from within.
Stirred harshly from the ashes,
An irreverent and ghostly wind.
It seeks the freshness and exuberance,
To rouse its tempest gales.
That feed the fiery winds of war,
In need of youth, it craves.
Thrown down upon the battlefields,
Like seeds sown on the wind.
No time for roots to hold,
For as the flames of war arise,
They scorch their fragile wings.
Causing them to tumble down,
Among the ashes once again.
Only to be resurrected,
When winds of war seek cause.

James P. Grigg
Danvers, MA

Things I Miss

Family birthday parties
Walking in mud puddles
Picnics on tablecloths laid out on the ground
Playing jack rocks on the sidewalk on a sunny June day
Christmas with all the family gathered around
Respect for parents and teachers who
Were wonderful role models
Afternoons of bliss doing nothing but skating or riding
A bicycle with the wind in your face
And racing through your hair
Sunday dinners made by Grandmother
No worries—and you were fed, clothed and your
Skinned knees were patched up
And getting old never entered your mind and you never
Had to ask yourself—where has my life gone?
What happened to my life?
And God was not questioned, just accepted by faith

Shirley Westbury
Richmond, VA

I am retired and an amateur poet who has not produced a lot of poems but I love to write. I am very glad for the encouragement of Eber & Wein Publishing and a certain Pastor Jim and a certain college professor Daisy. I never had any real writing training, so I just write from my heart and life experiences. It is very important for everyone to have avenues of expression. Our world will be better!

Untitled

I woke up that day, tired and lost,
but determined to get to work at any cost.
I walked out the door with a cold iced tea,
next thing I knew my car was kissing a tree.

I opened my eyes and saw friends all around.
I asked myself just what had gone down.
They told me I fainted and that's why I crashed.
The car was wrecked, my face pretty well smashed.

Now four long weeks later I'm coming around.
It's been a long road, but one thing I've found
is be grateful for health, family and friends.
They'll see you through anything right to the end.

Megan K. Noyes
Maynard, MA

With extreme gratitude, love and appreciation, this poem is dedicated to my loving parents, Lloyd, Jessica and Jeff. Thank you!

Hope

Hope is an interesting thing
Makes people do many thing
Many times that is what keeps us alive
The hope for the good things in our life

People can hope for many things
From smaller to much bigger things
People can hope for what they don't have
Or can hope to keep what they already have

Sometimes life brings you what you have asked for
Sometimes faith brings you what you have hoped for
In some cases it comes when you are not ready for it
In some cases it stays till you will be ready for it

When life brings it sometimes you don't see it
When you see it, sometimes you don't believe it
The hope is worthless without belief
In this one I strongly believe

I'm hoping to find the happiness in my life
I'm hoping to find a special one into my life
Special one with whom we can share the joy
With whom we can live a life that we enjoy

I believe that I have found the special one
For whom I was hoping for: the one
I'm hoping that we find the happiness together
I believe we will live our lives happily together

Zsigmond Torok
Dawa Point, CA

Winter Rose

Winter rose
Queen of the snow
Always so fair
You've had your share

Winter rose
Protector in white
Always on guard
Letting go can be hard

Winter rose
Faded memory now
Always somewhere inside
It's your time to hide

Winter rose
You cannot linger
She takes your place
Red rose her grace

Katie Lea
Brandon, MS

Dedication to Lana Lynne Dowell

My gratitude for merciful death is too profound to relate.
My comfort from fellow humans is too heartwarming for words.
My sympathy for loved ones is too heartfelt for conveyance.
The missing place too empty to fill.
The silent presence too silent to mourn.
My grief far, far too deep to voice.
My sorrow too consuming for tears.
My anguish too personal for lament.
My despair too consuming for tears.
The gap between life and death too wide to bridge —
Yet, her and God's presence are close.

Even so there is a reason. God needs sweet and good children in
heaven. As Hannah gave her child to God I could never do of my
own free will.

Since God chose to gently take my baby so be it. Now it is my
Christian duty to turn my grief into a Christian victory. I will give
her memory to all who accept it.

Too many times we humans become petty and unhappy. We take
life's good things for granted. We forget God. A few days of God's
blessings, care, happiness, and security are worth far more than a
lifetime of unhappiness.

I wish for all who accept the memory of Lana Lynne to remember
that all things spiritual, physical or material are gifts of God,
strive to make each day a happy one. Rejoice and be grateful to
God for all your blessings.

Betty L. Dowell
Manton, MI

For Lisa McCoy

You made a difficult journey
into a life that's new…
you didn't walk alone, my friend…
we walked it with you too.

The road we traveled ended
at Heaven's pearly gates,
and thought we would have followed
God said we'd have to wait.

You asked for us to carry on
to be strong our whole life through,
you knew we'd meet again one day
right now, God just needs you.

How sad it was to watch you go
how brave you fought the fight,
how peaceful it must have been
when you walked into the light.

We'll miss your beautiful smile
and your sweet, loving ways,
we'll cherish all the memories
we made along the way.

We'll try to face each new day
with grace, in all we do.
Knowing that everything changes
except our love for you.

Debbie Streitz
Everett, WA

Brain cancer took Lisa from us very quickly. She was brave and strong during her illness and never let it consume her. Her only concern was for those of us she left behind. I hope I can be as loving, kind and brave as Lisa when God decides to call me home. You may be gone from this life, but you will never be forgotten — we love you and miss you.

Untitled

A dull
Paynes grey
       Dawn
Over reaching
       All
Pendulously
Pregnantly
Storm heavy
Not a clearing
       Hope
Of a washed
       Out
Naples yellow
       Sun
In an instant
Heavenly
Cerulean blue
An orb of
Luminous orange
Warm shafts
Of a transparent
       Yellow
You arrived

Russ F. Housman
Arlington, VT

I have been a contributing artist with New York City galleries, shows and representation for years. Recovering from an accident, and not being in my studio for another month to continue the excitement of creativity, I have turned to poetry, to do with words what I can do with paint. I hope I can offer a different, conceptual view of what might be commonplace to some — a creative, conceptual view utilizing similar but different receptive senses.

The Rose

Of all the flowers that God made,
The yellow rose must have been
His most favorite flower of all:
So beautiful with long stems.

Petals soft like velvet;
Colors in so many hues.
They bring such joy into our lives,
With scent of sweet perfume.

They say "I love you" at your wedding,
"Hope you feel better" when you're not well,
"Goodbye" when your life is over
And with God you soon shall dwell.

So when my time on earth is over
And at last I am at rest,
All I want is a yellow rose
To lay softly on my breast.

When my eyes are closed forever
And roses I'll no more see,
Just one thing is all I ask for:
A yellow rose to take with me.

Sarah Tuttle
Wellington, OH

The Dream Has Gone

Poor, poor children, they're all undone
They married each other and had daughters and sons
They each thought they knew just who they got
But marriage proved they assuredly did not

They each married their heart's precious dream
Only to discover it was not as it seemed
What started as love's grand gift of life
Became bitterness and disappointment 'midst sorrow and strife

One is a plodder, easy going, just so
Drives the other crazy who's always on the go
Control, control and managing others
The flame of love it often smothers

Through life they go unhappy and mad
Robbed of the happiness they thought they had
Divorce is out of the question for them
Keeping up appearances is mighty slim

So be careful young lovers, dismiss not the quirks
That later will have you calling each other jerks
Step back a moment and assess those traits
Dreams disappear only after it's too late

Nancy J. Medlin
Chesapeake, VA

*I live with my family in Chesapeake, Virginia, and have been writing poems
for forty years. I often write about my surroundings, something that's touched
my heart or observations of life and how people deal with circumstances. This
particular poem touches on the sadness of a dream that has dissolved.*

Time's Unwinding

A clock ticks as time goes by
Time's unwinding, I don't know why
A brand new day at sunrise
To brighten the day a star in the sky
Gathered together, we are as one
To end the darkness, the rising sun
Start the beginning, start the day
Time's unwinding, as it fades away
Night falls once again
Another day over the sun descends
Darkness falls
Time's unwinding, another sunrise
And the light is blinding
Never to end, much too fast
Day and night time will pass
A peaceful calm, a clock will run
Keeping the darkness from the sun
Time sets another night
No way to stop it, no way to fight
A sunrise as time goes by
And sets again to darken the sky
Time's unwinding, I don't know why
A beautiful night,
From the stars in the sky
Time's unwinding

Steve Adams
Sacramento, CA

I've been blessed writing. I hope you enjoy it too. I work construction during the day and write the weekends through. I'm teaching myself how to write, doing a job I didn't know I was working on, writing all day or till the sun rose again. Writing is a passion and truly a joy, writing because it's a choice and time is unwinding. Thank you all and God bless.

Chalk

City streets are often covered in chalk.
Sometimes it is obscene graffiti.
Occasionally it is beautiful art.
My apartment building's street corner is like that,
But its chalk usually takes on a hopscotch pattern.
Most afternoons and evenings little girls play there.
They laugh and giggle and have so much fun!

Today that corner sidewalk is also covered in chalk,
But the hopscotch design has vanished now.
Another drawing has taken its place:
The outline of the body
Of a ten-year-old girl
Killed accidentally in a drive-by shooting.
No one is laughing today.

Robert P. Tucker
Lakeland, FL

During my years as a graduate student at the University of Chicago Divinity School, I often read of such dreadful deaths in that city. I wrote this poem about one of them in my neighborhood. It was so tragic and so unnecessary. I grieved, though I did not know the child. It is my hope that we may all work together to make such horrible events a thing of the past.

Blossoms in the Springtime

Blossoms in the sunshine,
Give my heart a lift.
The sight of pretty petals
To me is a great gift.

Purple is the lilac,
Pink the cherry tree,
Mimosa is all yellow,
As bright as you can see.

Scents they are all varied,
The hyacinth is sweet,
Jonquils smell like lilies,
Skunk cabbage smells like feet.

Tulip trees are proud and tall,
Violets they are little,
Snowdrops, they are also small,
Hawthorn is in the middle.

Oft indoors I'll close my eyes,
I'll see these wondrous flowers.
I'll sniff and even smell their scents
And feel their healing powers.

So when your life seems knotted up,
Sit quietly and see,
If you too can imagine,
God's gift to you and me.

Vanessa A. S. Evans
San Diego, CA

The Lambeau Mystique Stands

The opening kick off every fall of the green and gold
never gets old. The Lambeau Mystique has grown
with the launch zones, hands down, for Lambeau leaps
into the end zone seats celebrating every Packer touch down.

It is either Lombardi time or Tardy time in title town.
Timing the time of sacred space at the right time and place:
In a tale of two halves, time is of the essence we do not have.

Lambeau Field is the crown jewel of the NFL shield.
Ergo: one 24-hour, 24-carat green and golden day;
Four quarters of one power packed hour of play
Studded with 60 ruby minutes—each minute capped
With 60 diamond seconds on display Sundays.

Go pack—the pack attack wins at home in Lambeau
As their opponents around the league well know.
Front and center—fans know when the pack own
Field position and time of possession, man-to-man,
They are winning the battle in the trenches,
And that can be a matter of inches in the pros.

The Green Bay Packer second brain, Lambeau field—
Supposing it to be a primitive facility, win every down
On the ground by pounding the rock and winding down the clock.

After four spiraling quarters of good sound football,
The Packers defend the NFL shield with their sum total
Of good play—at a Packer game in the Green Bay
Second brain, Lambeau field, hey-hey!

Jeffrey Cameron
Green Bay, WI

*I live poor well in Green Bay, Wisconsin. I enjoy the waters of the Bay of Green
Bay and the awesome Lake Michigan. I followed the legendary Green Bay Packers
of Curly Lambeau to Vince Lombardi, to the present. I followed the stars to Green
Bay, but I enjoy several other NFL teams in pro football. The north woods appeal
to me, although I visit larger metros regularly like Chicago and Milwaukee often.
I've taken the Evylin Wood speed reading and retention course that has helped me
write poetry. My favorite poet is the American poet Edgar Allan Poe.*

Rainy Day Pictures

It rained today I'm glad to say
But I couldn't go shopping
And the kids couldn't go out to play.
They would fight and squall
And just drive me up the wall
And I would shout:
Be quiet, stop that, cut it out.
But none of that did any good
So I decided to take pictures.
There were smiles, tears
And dirty faces, too.
It's simply amazing
What a few pictures can do.

Guyola Carr
Conroe, TX

Face of the Boulder

Thirty crazies has October
Then we look over our shoulder
To see some fun on the run
Or dates that have us colder.
For "our" loves are without
Gloves and always grow no
Older. And so when's Kepler
10-B that we've fantasied
And that's our story over.
While finding siding spring's
Clout, a love with a pout
Will be on the face of
The boulder.

Leroy J. Fairfield
New Port Richey, FL

Over our shoulder is a reference to 1908 meteor reaction Tugunsta, because the very next sized, timed one is February 15, 2013, Russia again. Fantasized about Kepler 10-B is a reference to a stone cut relief of a plant in between two ancient Sumerians, the plant of knowledge. Those who grow no older are the ones who put comet siding spring near Mars on October 19, 2014, but an inch closer to something else on October 20, 2014.

Mother

The rose of my life is my mother,
For in this world there is no other.
She is sweet, and a true friend to the end.
The one on whom I can always depend.
Her gentle touch, her kind embrace,
Hers is a life filled with love and grace.
The rose's beauty shall never fade
For life for her is the one God made.

Ralph Whitley
Concord, NC

I Sing the Body Electric

The discharge of blood,
from body cavity,
something unique to female humans,
and other animals, of the female species.
The break and tear of uterine walls.
Saying you are now a woman,
    or at the least, blessed with the act of conceiving.
      Connecting you to the earth.
You are one of, you are a mother to us all.

Wayne Jackson
San Francisco, CA

For M. B., I occasionally made her laugh, with a joke, which dried her tears, over those many years. She was born on December 13, 1947 and died August 3, 2010.

If She and He Could

If she could she would give you
the world if she could. Because
she knows if you could, you would
give her the best of everything
in the world. And him too.
But both of you know you have
to wait for *paradise* soon.
Since the one up above
can, could, would, and
will and for all the coulds,
and woulds in the world,
remember the one up above
will bring *paradise*.
Paradise will be *"all"* roses
and wildflowers to me. If he
could he would but he
can't so just forget it.
He always says, "Eat
the fat of the land."
So does *the one up above*.
That is why he is bringing
paradise to the
world internationally
soon,
according to His *timetable*.

Priscilla Thomas
Tampa, FL

Nature's Beauty

Fields of wildflowers blowing softly in the wind
Turtles swimming and sunning in a pond
Hearing a woodpecker high in a tree
Squirrels scattering and chattering here and there
Butterflies fluttering from flower to flower
Birds singing and chirping their sweet songs
Small lizards running across the path
The winds are rustling the leaves
Making their own kind of music
Discoveries all around
Nature can teach us about life
And finding beauty, joy and stillness all around

Veronica Durre
Long Beach, CA

The River of Life

Our song was "Moon River," we listened to it play.
 We knew we'd be together and make the trip one day.
The day we married, our trip began.
 We were on the river, enjoying it as it ran.
The flow was smooth and gentle as we drifted along,
 Just like "Moon River," the river of the song.
We had two children along the way.
 We loved them and enjoyed them every day.
The children now have grown, they have moved on.
 We're back on the river again, since they are gone.
The flow has quickened, we are going faster.
 I have the feeling we're heading toward disaster.
There's a loud sound just up ahead.
 My heart is anxious, so full of dread.
The day you died, we went over the fall.
 I didn't know what to do, I could hear heaven call.
It didn't take long, I knew they were calling you.
 I couldn't let you go, I wanted to go too.
I was swept over the falls, going along with the flow.
 You were gone, I ended in the turbulence below.
We all have guardian angels, now you'll be my guide,
 Leading me through my life, always by my side.
One day I'll find the end, I'll wash up on the shore.
 My life will be over, I'll ride the river no more.
I'll see you at the rainbow's end, you'll wait for me.
 We can be together again, for all eternity.

Janice Smith
Harrisonville, MO

My husband and I met in March of 1961. When we dated, the song "Moon River" would play on the radio. As I listened, I was dreaming about living my life with him. Two years later, we married. He had joined the Army, so we were able to see some of the world together. He developed cancer and together we fought a hard battle. We lost the battle in October of 2012. He was seventy-one when he died. Since then, I have written several poems. I entered one last year. The poem is titled "The River of Life."

The Prodigal

My son, take hold of my hand
Return to Me, and follow my commands.
Though you have sinned,
I will still forgive,
Though you have strayed,
I will still save.

I have watched you grow,
From a boy into a man,
Allow me son,
To guide you and to stand.

I have loved you, with an everlasting love,
And I have prayed for you,
From Heaven's seat above.

My son, take hold of my hand
Return to Me, and follow my commands.
You once were lost, but now, you are found,
Return to Me, and be heaven-bound…

My son, take hold of my hand

JoAnn Gallagher
Inverness, FL

I wrote this poem, "The Prodigal," many years ago, originally as a song and then converted it to a poem. I wrote it with my oldest son in mind, since he was away from the Lord, at the time. I prayed for him for many years as I did for all my sons. Then, about four years ago, he called me to tell me he accepted Christ back into his heart. I never shared this poem with him, but I am so happy God heard my prayers and placed someone in his path to minister the word and lead him back to God. I have been writing poetry for many years as well as writing many songs. Writing has always come easy to me and I enjoy doing it. I have been married for twenty-eight years. We reside in Inverness, Florida, but we're originally from Long Island, New York. All our children are married, and we have one grandson and three granddaughters.

My Greatest Story of All

When I was young
So many years ago
There was a story to tell
That I was yet to know
Of two young men so strong and true
One dressed in red, the other in blue
They face the world, eyes wide, straight on
To serve and protect
The city from harm
Even as children they would go the extra mile
To help when they could to lend a hand with a smile
The older one a father of boys, there are two
Saw the 9/11 tragedy fresh out of school
The other a young man who lost friends of his own
Those wounds to their hearts
Some the deepest they've known
Though they are grown now, still with dreams to be met
The pride and the love in my heart is so set
My two young men who grew strong and tall
My heroes, my sons
My greatest story of all

Joan Sullivan
Monroe Township, NJ

Will You Be "Mist?"

When you have seen three score and ten,
    It's time to think of where you've been;
What people drew your love or scorn?
    Had some wished you were never born?

A life with purpose—that's the goal,
    So make it so, with heart and soul.
Our legacy is ours to make,
    And we must learn what route to take.

When we are gone, will we be missed
    On leaving from the living list?
It may depend, e'er we depart,
    On when and where we touch a heart.

Or were our "footsteps in the sand"
    Erased by an all-knowing hand?
While we still breathe we should resist
    A foggy fate that ends in mist.

"Do unto others…"—that's the way
    To guide your actions day by day.
If we do more than just exist,
    Our lives leave more than merely mist.

Jim O. Berkland
Glen Ellen, CA

During my eighty-five years, I have written more than one thousand poems for family, co-workers, and just for myself, when the muse strikes me. (Perhaps it merely amuses me.) In reviewing several unpublished catalogs of my poetic works, this one, "Will You Be 'Mist?,'" seemed especially appropriate at this stage of my life, to pass along to kindred souls. Innermost feelings of love, philosophy and religious needs seem best expressed by poetry and I hope that others will appreciate what I consider to be one of my best efforts.

The Lonely Man

He was a lonely man
sitting on a bench, hat in his hand.
His face was sad, his clothes were shabby,
a look of sorrow in his eyes.
Hoping some kind soul would stop
perhaps to drop a dollar or some change
into his empty hat.
As I approached, he looked up,
a smile on his lips.
"Good morning," he said,
"Could you spare a dime?"
I looked at him and saw a man,
a veteran, down on his luck.
Instead of a dime, I bought him lunch
in gratitude for his service.
Wishing I could do more
for someone so deserving,
I gave him a five, wished him luck
and went about my day.

Alice Hill
Renton, WA

Lost Love

where do we go when love goes away
when our heart is left with sorrow and woe
the days are bleak and the nights are long
our mind is left wondering what went wrong

all around us the world goes on
except in our hearts there is no song
we can't find an answer we may never know why
where do we go when love says goodbye

we live with the sadness with each passing day
wondering why love had to go away
hold the ones you love close to your heart
for the day may come when you have to part

live each day like it may be the last
for in the end you cannot change the past
someday in the future you may have to say
where will I go now that love's gone away

Betty J. Russell
Cleveland, TN

My husband of forty-seven years encourages me to write. He is my best friend, my love and my life. This poem was written in memory of the special people, who have touched my life through the years, that I have lost. My faith in God gets me through everything.

Savor the Moment

Dishes stacked high, but it doesn't matter
Remnants of food on every platter
Toys scattered here and there
Disarray everywhere
The laughter loud and spirits high
How blessed we are, I thought with a sigh
The family's together, recalling the past
My oh my, time passes so fast
After the clutter and toys are stored away
We will always remember this Thanksgiving day

Bev Levine
Cincinnati, OH

At eighty-eight years old and widowed, there is no greater joy than being surrounded by my loving family. It is to my children, grandchildren and great-grandchildren that I dedicate this poem.

Back Breaker

Cracking knees,
Baggy eyes.
Body aches,
Soul cries.
Hour by hour the work drags on
Always tired, days so long.

Numb fingers, swollen knees,
Bad back, no reprieve.
Sick men in rooms, heaped.
Oppressor in van, sleeps.
Not fair, no voice,
And you think this was his choice.

No light at the end of the tunnel,
Golden years down the funnel.
Work yourself until you die,
Nothing to show. Why, oh why?
You can't get out, you can't escape
This desperate, lower-middle class state.

I take this chance to ask you now…
America tell me how,
A man can work until bloody and beat,
And still can't afford to make end's meat.

Tom Folske
Stacy, MN

Set Free

There is a prison, its walls are high and wide,
And I am there because of sinful "I."

Jesus saw me there and cried,
Come out my child, for I have died.

I paid the penalty, I paid the price,
There is no need to pay it twice.

Ask me, trust me, and I will come in,
And cleanse your heart from sin!

And set you free,
So you can spend eternity with me.

There is no prison now for me,
For my eyes are open and now I see.

Jesus gave His life for me,
The price was paid upon a tree.

Accept this truth and be like me,
Set free from sin, set free!

The Bible says to you and me,
The truth will make you free indeed!

Jesus died for you and me,
Oh, how can it be?
Jesus' love so full and free,
From death, has rescued you and me!

Dolores Livingstone
Fayette City, PA

I'm seventy-seven years old, and I'm thrilled to share Jesus with so many people! This is the first poem Jesus gave to me when he said to me, "Write!" He gave this poem to me immediately. He still gives me poems everyday! I have many books full of them. His words are all perfect and righteous. I'm praying that they make an impact on your life. Trust and love Him, because He really does love you!

Most of Us Are Poets

I think most of us are poets, secretly
When we touch the face of our lover
The world glows in a new light
Hearts explode in great crescendos of hope
Words form but cannot be spoken
Through the fluttering breaths like excited doves
So the poems go unwritten, but instead are felt
The poet is secretly there

I think most of us are poets, undiscovered
Raising our fists with words
Demanding honest politicians
Advocating equality and justice
Learning early on that freedom isn't truly free
Opening the eyes of others with ideas, thoughts, words
Everyone can make an impact
Anyone can alter the world

I think most of us are poets, straining
When we take a moment to connect
With a person, place, thing, our life
Changes, shifts in a slightly new direction, lifts off,
Pollen in the wind, a chance to grow, to start again
Form a new experience into feelings
Those feelings into words
Now we have the poet and the poetry

Paige Lauren Dillard
Lakeside, CA

Paige Lauren Dillard is in school to become a librarian. She has three self-published books sold on Amazon.com including a book of poetry. She would like to dedicate this poem to anyone who has ever been moved by a moment so special, or a love so special, that they wanted to share their experience with everyone. She also encourages everyone to pick up a pen and write, for she knows words can change the world.

Textation

Heads down, thumbs moving
In a rapid pace,
Scrolling on a little box
With no face-to-face.

One can be smiling,
Or have a frightful frown,
But thumbs are still moving
With heads bent lowly down.

Oh yes, the modern way,
For a direct converse,
But to talk face-to-face
Can still be truly terse.

Dennis E. Lockette
Columbia, MO

There are many positive aspects about our modern day communicative technology, but I wrote this poem as a critique on some of the negative aspects, as I personally observed and what people tell me at their family gatherings. The most common observation is a relative or friend, and not necessarily a teen, constantly texting, for either business or personal pleasure, or just playing games on their phones. Hopefully, the ability to carry on a decent conversation face-to-face, without that little box, will not be a lost art.

More to Do

Yum! Pizza's done!
What fun!
At four score plus two,
There's lots more I want to do.

Don't close the door on Great-Grandma yet!
I've many more games to play, you bet!

A bit of tennis with old rackets of mine,
Still shout out to me, "Pancho Gonzales!"
So great in his time.

Want to play a set or two?
Not the way we used to do!
Huff, puff, and laugh all day,
Now, it's about one hour then, "Hit the hay!"

Good games, they say, keep the "old" bugs away!
That's just what I dream for me,
There's lots more I want to see.

To sing and dance on stage sounds great!
What's the next Senior Club Talent Show date?

We'll get some laughs, there'll be no frowns,
We'll surely act like a bunch of clowns.
I'll drink cool water and nothing stronger,
'Cause I want to drive home and live a lot longer!

Barbara J. Brown
Santa Maria, CA

Christmas Cactus

(which only blooms in July)

a single bloom
which lit the room
despite colored lights on the tree
a gesture fair
who couldn't but stare
at the gentle bud now set free
a sight so pleasant
that special Christmas present
which united our whole family
there was no snow
but Mom let us know
she'd be with us eternally

Terry Dion
Ridge, NY

Spring

The wind is blowing
    As I look outside
Trees are swaying
    Having a ride
Birds are appearing
    Flying high in the sky
Looking for a place to land
    Hope it will be close by
It is time for them all
    To find a place to rest
Gather sticks and twigs
    For making a nest
Clouds are forming in
    The western sky
Storm, wind or rain or
    Will it just pass by
Only the Lord knows what
    It will be
He is in control at all times
    Is easy to see

Dorothy Huls
Beatrice, NE

Slips of Pink

We're told that pink is "color of the year."
Then shout "hurrah" for pastel sweeps of dawn,
For bright flamingo lakes afar, and here
Their comic cousins on the neighbor's lawn.
Salute the hollyhocks that bravely stand,
The spent petunias lolling on the grass,
The tiny seashells winking in the sand
And gathered now in pink Depression glass.
Keep watch for grosbeaks, their plump breasts ablaze,
Crab apple petals billowing on the breeze,
The beaks of female cardinals, and the sprays
Of summersweet that tantalize the bees.
    And special cheers for consolation sips
    Of rosé wine, for fingertips… and lips!

Cynthia Newgarden
Plattsburgh, NY

Your Smiling Face

Your smiling face is my sunshine
It rained the other day
Your warmth and beauty brightened
Through
And chased the clouds away
Your glowing eyes, your tenderness
Your warmth and kindness, too
All help me to realize
Why I'm so fond of you
And should some clouds appear
Again
And darken my sunlight skies
I'll think of you
And you alone
And watch the clouds drift by

John Van Ness
Tuxedo, NY

Wisdom of Gandhi

leader of India
small of stature
guided by compassion
loyalty did capture

humbled by photo
of his possessions
handful of basics
held my attention

with spinning wheel
to make cloth
spectacles to read
bowl for broth

pair of sandals
carved monkeys three
all rejecting evil
hear speak see

obey British authority
he willfully refused
to secure independence
non-violence was used

Marc Miceli
Nalcrest, FL

The following are a few favorite quotations. "Non-violence is the first article of my faith. It is also the last article of my creed." "In my humble opinion, non-cooperation with evil is as much a duty as is cooperation with good." "What difference does it make to the dead, the orphans and the homeless, whether the mad destruction is wrought under the name of totalitarianism or the holy name of liberty or democracy?" "The moment the slave resolves that he will no longer be a slave, his fetters fall. He frees himself and shows the way to others. Freedom and slavery are mental states."

Hello World—How Lucky Am I

To sit under the billowing trees
    nature shares with us
The fragrance of flowers
    blooming
Birds singing softly
    through the wind ever so graceful
Listening to the trees
    call to them as they gently flow
To breathe in the air
    that has life all around us
Knowing that you
    are not alone
But one with the world
    how lucky am I
The freedom to roam
    to feel life
How lucky am I
    to reach out to others
In good health or in pain
    being a friend to someone who needs you
Only to be rewarded
    by a smile and a
Thank you
Now go out and see
    that you can be
The one to say—how lucky am I

Lucia Coffman
Manhattan, KS

God's Wonderful Creation

In all of creation we see the hand of God:

The beautiful rainbow that spans the sky above
shows the promise of God's wondrous love.
The birds that float upon the air
sing sweetly of God's loving care.
The winds whisper His holy name
and all of creation proudly proclaims
that our wonderful and gracious God
created the whole earth on which we trod.

Our loving God watches over us day and night
and always helps us do what is right.
With joy we sing of His glory.
We love to proclaim His story
to all on earth who will hear,
to everyone, far away and near
that God loves and blesses us all:
His loving creation, both great and small.

Debora Robbins
Temple, TX

I am Debora Robbins. I am fifty-five years old and single. I am a member of the Church of Christ in Temple, TX. My hobbies include writing poetry and songs and reading my Bible, other books and magazines. I also love doing things on my computer. I would like to dedicate this poem to all my family and friends, who have supported me throughout the years, and most especially to God, my Father, and my Lord and Savior Jesus Christ who are my all in all.

God's Unending Love

As I reflect life's earthly journey, I can't help but wonder why,
    All the pitfalls God allowed me only strengthened and advised
All the laughter, joy and heartaches, every tear God wiped away,
    Was an answered prayer I offered, God alone knows what to say.

God was always right beside me helping make decisions right,
    All the answers to my future were designed by God's delight;
All my fears and doubts subside as God's promises come to mind,
    I can never here repay Him for the blessings that are mine.

When I survey the wondrous Cross and my debt of sin He paid,
    I can never, ever fail Him, at the Cross my sins were laid;
My life with loved ones dear, He has filled my every need,
    The ending of life's journey will be beautiful indeed.

Don't forget what's most important when your life is passing by,
    Put your trust in God, the Father, He alone can satisfy;
At the ending of your journey, God's gift of peace will suffice,
    He is all we need to enter Heaven's glorious paradise.

God's love is unending, unconditional and sure,
    He never stops trying to make our life pure;
You'll never regret making God first in your life,
    When you rest at night knowing everything is all right.

Maxine L. Felty
Clermont, FL

My father, Leon Lewis, was a music lover who authored several hymns published in hymn books of Stamps Baxter and James D. Vaughan Publishers. By age five, he could see I had a talent that needed to be channeled in ministry and began my piano lessons. With his relentless interest, he began shaping my life for a vocation that has proved to be extremely rewarding. His parental guidance led to my accomplishments of twenty-three years employment in church ministry as administrative secretary and also church organist. The gift of poetry is the icing on the cake.

Christmas

Christ is in Christmas for a reason
We all know why we have this season
The star in the heaven shined real bright
For this one fine and glorious night
And no one had a reason to fright
The three wise men stayed by the stable
Knowing Christ had no cradle
And was not given milk from a ladle
The lamb and sheep slept by his side
And no one ever heard a cry
Baby Jesus had a bed of hay
And this is where he had to lay
While everyone else kneeled and prayed

James Carrigan
Ft. Worth, TX

Life Is a Journey

'Tis a little journey,
this we walk.
Hardly time for murmurs
time for talk.
Sometimes happiness,
sometimes tears.
Often loses felt
for years.
Yet, God's love can
comfort our fears.
Yes, life is a journey,
soon goes by.
Let's you and I
be friends e're we die.

Dot Karnes
Little Rock, AR

Index of Poets